Author's Preface

I have spent all of my 56 deer seasons hunting out of the same hunting camp and wouldn't have it any other way. Although I've read numerous books and magazines about white-tailed deer hunting, I've noted that very little is ever mentioned about the activities that go on in hunting camps after the hunt is concluded, what it takes to make a deer camp function successfully, the importance of actually belonging to a deer hunting camp, and all the effort that it takes to make a hunting camp thrive and to endure through the generations.

The reader should find some interesting deer hunting stories contained herein, but this is not just another book about white-tailed deer hunting. My goal is to relate to the reader that the deer hunt is actually only a small portion of what it means to gather together every fall and attempt to shoot a huge buck. To all of us who hunt out of a deer camp or belong to a hunting group, the primary purpose of deer hunting is, indeed, much more than tramping the woods to shoot a deer. The hunt is about gathering each fall with the same people year after year to share the bond that develops between father and son, family members, friends, and other hunters with whom one has the privilege of sharing the woods. The memories, the stories that are told time and time again, the fellowship, the camaraderie, the laughter, the thrill of the hunt, and the time one is able to spend away from the normal routine of daily life and to reacquaint oneself with all of the joys of nature are just as important as the hunt itself. This is a story about a successful hunting camp that continues to perpetuate because of the rules and traditions established by the "Jolly Boys" when they organized their deer hunting camp in the mid-1950s. I am hopeful that everyone who reads this book will have a dream of someday establishing their own "Blue Heaven" and that the information provided in this book will help them to make their own hunting camp a success.

ACKNOWLEDGEMENTS

I am dedicating this book to my father and the four other men who called themselves the "Jolly Boys" and to the deer hunting camp they called "Blue Heaven." This is their story and legacy, and it wouldn't have been possible without the encouragement and skillful editing by my wife, Kathryn Mortwedt-Hanson, my sister-in-law Dianne Mortwedt-Kramer, and Dianne's close friend and accomplished editor, Mary Rogers. These ladies were all instrumental in making the story more readable and engaging. Special thanks to these women whose lives have been all about reading and writing.

Prologue

In the mid-1950s, Sawyer County, along with many other counties in Wisconsin, began to issue recreational use permits on a first-come, first-served basis to people who wanted to construct a hunting cabin on county forestland for the purpose of hunting.

These permits were allowed based on Wisconsin State Statute 28.11, which authorized Sawyer County and the other counties in the state to provide recreational opportunities to the public. The statute was very vague, and, as a result, Sawyer County began issuing the permits for hunting cabins at a cost of $10.00 per year but limited the number of permits to 100.

The permit allowed the "permittee" to "rent" county forest land on which to place the hunting cabin. The guidelines for the size of the cabin were dictated by the county, and the cabin was not to be built on a permanent foundation. It was a conditional permit which required the permittee to "not cut any green timber, commit waste, or do any damage to the county forest lands." The only privilege given the permittee was to use the cabin for hunting purposes and to cut dead timber for the purpose of providing heat to the cabin. Although the permits were very restrictive, it was the ideal solution for many hunters in the area for establishing a hunting camp in the forest at an affordable cost.

Introduction

It was 1954 in Hayward, Wisconsin, and memories of World War II were still fresh in the minds of almost everyone. This was the "Greatest Generation," and people were optimistic, though many didn't have anything but their youth and the hard-earned belief that in America prosperity could belong to anyone who worked hard. That's what my father and his friends believed. Married to Violet Erickson, whom he met at the Smith Lake Pavilion while performing in the Jack Olson Orchestra, Marvin Hanson entered the Navy and returned to his home town of Hayward after the war ended. He was 37 years old, and he, my mother, my sister, Marilynn, and I, lived in a house on Fourth Street which he had built under the G.I. Bill.

For some time, my dad and several of his friends had talked about starting a deer hunting camp. Sometimes at my dad's grocery store, sometimes on Saturday or Sunday evenings when families would get together and "pass a dish" for a pot luck get-together, sometimes in the backyard, but most often while sitting around the kitchen table sipping on a beer, my dad, Merle Dunster, Kenneth Sugrue,

Howard Nystrom, and Alvin "Adder" Madson would talk about their dream of building a hunting camp. That dream would become a reality in November 1955 and would become known as "Blue Heaven," named after the popular song "My Blue Heaven." Adder loved that song and suggested they call the camp by that name.

And the group of men who dreamed it, built it, and hunted it until the day they died called themselves the Jolly Boys. This is a recounting, as well as memories and written testimony allow, of their traditions, fellowship, camaraderie, and love of the hunt in the rustic atmosphere of a Wisconsin deer camp. This is the story of the legacy of one of Hayward's original hunting camps, which continues to live on, now more than half a century later.

I was ten years old in 1954, and life was a lot less complicated than it is today. We didn't own a television set. We couldn't afford one, and those who could found very little to watch on their TVs because Hayward was too far from any metropolitan area to get reception. Very little was purchased on credit back then. Everyone was trying to make ends meet with what they had. Everyone knew everyone else. Nobody locked their doors at night or when they were away. Everyone had one vehicle, and most were old clunkers, no longer capable of long trips. Very few cars had radios, so when you did go somewhere, you made your own entertainment by singing, which seemed to make the trip shorter. Children were always outside and entertained themselves with games of make-believe war or cowboys and Indians. We were never bored and neither were our parents. The adults entertained themselves by getting together with friends, relatives or neighbors. And there was always singing at the get-togethers. Everyone worked at least six days a week. Some worked even more. My parents owned a grocery store and were open from 7 a.m. until 7 p.m. or later in the evenings. On Sundays in the summer, they were open from 9 a.m. until 1 p.m.

Adults had little leisure time, but my parents would put together a party on very short notice. Frequently, one of the neighbors would stop by near supper time just to say hello and see what we were having for dinner. My mother would invite the neighbors and their family to join with us for dinner, or we would end up at their place for the evening. They would simply combine what was available and put it out on the table for everyone to enjoy. It was a sharing, caring time. When we did end up at someone else's home for dinner, my mother would always be certain that we invited those people back to our house as soon as possible to "pay them back." I recall my mother telling my father "We owe them."

It was against this 1950s background that the Jolly Boys were created. I have very enduring and vivid memories of the many meetings and conversations of the Jolly Boys as they made preparations to begin their project. They were a diverse group but had one common goal. When the opportunity to lease land from the county for the purpose of constructing a hunting camp became available, they all knew what they wanted: a hunting camp.

Their main focus was to decide where to put the hunting camp, how to find the money to construct and equip it, who would be allowed to hunt out of the camp, how they would heat it and provide electricity for lights, how to handle the finances for the supplies, rules of conduct, rules of ownership, and how to keep the camp alive. Many hunting camps failed and disbanded after being in existence for a short time.

The "Jolly Boys" (L-R): Howard Nystrom, Kenny Sugrue, Alvin "Adder" Madson, Marvin Hanson and Merle Dunster.

The Jolly Boys

Alvin "Adder" Madson, the oldest of the Jolly Boys, was probably about 44 at that time. He had worked almost his entire life at Peoples National Bank in Hayward in a variety of positions. He came honestly by his nickname, Adder, which stuck because of his number skills recognized by all who knew him. He was considered a strong community and church leader and was highly respected in Hayward's financial circles. His wife, Ellen, also worked at the bank as a teller. Together they raised three children in Hayward—Sue Ellen, Jay Peter, and Phillip—in a white cape cod with black shutters across from the Hayward Golf Course. It was considered at that time and even now to be a very nice part of town. Slight of build but assertive of opinion, Adder still maintained an open mind about the world. Adder was a soft-spoken man who took hunting and the hunting camp very seriously. His knowledge of other hunting camps in the area was vast, and he was looked to for much of the guidance as the Jolly Boys set about making their hunting camp. He had hunted out of many of these camps and had formulated a strong opinion on how one should be operated.

My father, Marvin "Marv" Hanson, was the son of Bernard Hanson, a well-known mercantiler who built and operated the Hanson Mercantile Company in Hayward. He worked at the store in his youth, acquiring a background in the grocery and butcher business which gave him the impetus to start his own business, Marv's Super Value, located where Tremblay's Fudge Shop now sits in downtown Hayward. My mother, Violet, worked at the grocery store too, ringing up groceries and checking out customers who were pretty much all on a first-name basis. As was the practice in those days—driven by practicality and need—the entire family helped out at such stores, so it was inevitable that my sister Marilynn and I also worked at the store. Marilynn helped to stock shelves, while I bagged groceries and carried them out to the customer's car.

Kenneth "Kenny" Sugrue was the mayor of Hayward at this time, and he also owned and operated his own gas station, located next to the Carnegie Library on Highway 63. He was married to Norma, whom everyone called "Puffin." They had a daughter named Margaret, whom they called "Dolly." Although Kenny was a Jolly Boy, he didn't hunt or own a deer rifle. But he badly wanted to be a part of this new hunting camp. He also didn't drink anything but ginger ale, a trait that no doubt should have excluded him immediately from the camp. However the Jolly Boys liked him and appreciated his mechanical skills which were well known in the area and were sorely needed for the jeeps that provided the transportation in and out of Blue Heaven. Although Kenny never hunted, this curly-haired, well-built man possessed a remarkably sweet, soft, and mellow baritone voice and could sing with the best of them. People could not believe the sound that came out of that man, and the Jolly Boys and their friends loved to sing. Song, in those days, was a major form of entertainment for everyone. And it was self-produced.

Howard Nystrom was a trim and fit man, a Standard Oil distributor for Hayward in those years, delivering fuel oil and gasoline to his customers at homes and businesses. He and his wife, Elva, had two children, Dale and Debbie. The Jolly Boys always worried about Howard's smoking habit because he frequently fell asleep in his bunk at Blue Heaven with a lit cigarette still in his hand. Quick-witted, social, and handsome with a perpetual smile on his face, Howard loved to hunt. But his great fondness for Blue Heaven was in the evening card games and the drinks that were poured as dinner was being prepared on the wood-burning stove. Howard passed away in his late forties of a heart attack, not too many years after the establishment of the hunting camp.

Merle Dunster was the youngest of the Jolly Boys and, without a doubt, the most colorful and charming of the group. He was my father's first cousin and also my father's brother-in-law, married to my mother's sister, Gloria, a glamorous, fun-loving lady known for her beautiful blonde hair. They had two children, Barbara and John Kimball, or "JK," as he was known, as there were just too many Johns in the family. At the time, Merle was working for Mrs. Sutliff, who owned three lumber yards in Hayward, Stone Lake, and Cable.

Merle worked at all three lumber yards, and that relationship would become very critical as the hunting camp was built. Although Merle was an excellent carpenter and hunter, his skills were somewhat overshadowed by his antics at Blue Heaven. These included a performance as a Russian Dancer one evening in which a plate full of spaghetti on the table was kicked into the air, coating everyone at the table in spaghetti sauce. He also spent many evenings wearing Groucho Marx glasses to distract the other card players from concentrating on the game. He was always the first to put together an evening of song and performance.

Merle Dunster, enjoying a cigar and peppermint schnapps following an evening poker game, and wearing his "Groucho" glasses to disguise his identity.

PERMIT FOR CAMP #52

It was easy for the men to decide they wanted a hunting camp, it was easy to name it "Blue Heaven," and it was easy to call themselves—what else?—the "Jolly Boys."

Less easy were decisions regarding location, design, site preparation, legal ownership, building materials, costs, and how the camp would be run. From the beginning, nothing was taken lightly in terms of decision-making. The Jolly Boys knew that underneath the deceptively innocent names "Jolly Boys" and "Blue Heaven" lay great responsibility that would require fairness, equal labor and input, and consensus on many, many issues, some that would not even become clear until the camp was operating.

Adder, who had spent considerable time hunting out of various other hunting camps, had witnessed many of them fail. He had seen relationships ruined and families split over things that should have been fleshed out early in the camps' beginnings. He insisted that the Jolly Boys take heed, and they did.

I recall that in the early winter deer season of 1954 my dad, along with Merle, Adder, Howard, and several others, went hunting on county forest land about a half mile north of Nelson Lake—an area known as the Totagatic Flowage. It was a remote area with high rolling hills containing maple, yellow birch, oak, and basswood trees, with many tag alder and cedar swamps, making it an area that most hunters would regard as big buck country. My father was walking on an old, abandoned logging road when he came upon two eight-point bucks running side by side as they came over the crest of a hill parallel to him and headed toward the protection of a large cedar swamp. My father, a skilled hunter with a Winchester Model 94 .30-30, shot both deer. My father always referred to those bucks as "twins," but that day he decided that those twins were a sign that this was where the hunting camp should be built. The other Jolly Boys readily agreed, and Adder was assigned the task of getting a permit from the Sawyer County Forestry Department to build the camp in this area. Adder found the precise location in the plat book, and on March 7, 1955, Camp 52 was born.

PERMIT FOR HUNTING CAMP

This Indenture made and concluded this 7th day of March 19 55 by and between Sawyer County, a municipal corporation, with its seat of government at Hayward, Wisconsin, hereinafter called the Permitter and Alvin Madson Hayward, Wisconsin hereinafter called the Permittee.

WITNESSETH that the said Permitter, subject to and in compliance with the conditions hereinafter specified, hereby authorizes the Permittee to erect a cabin to be used for hunting purposes on the following described land, to-wit:

SW¼ of the SE¼ of Section 16, Township 42 North, Range 9 West

This Permit is for the term of one year from January 1, 19 55 to January 1 19 56 . Permittee is to pay an annual rent of Ten Dollars ($10.00), to be paid to Permitter at the time of execution and delivery of this Permit.

Permittee shall have the privilege of cutting such dead timber as is necessary to be used for firewood to heat the hunting cabin, but shall not cut any green timber or commit waste.

This Permit may be terminated at once by Permitter, if Permittee commits waste or damage on said property.

Permitter may hold the cabin and retain it for its own to compensate for any damages to said property, if any such damage is committed. If the real estate hereinbefore described is renewed at the expiration of this Permit, Permittee shall have first option to renew it. Permittee may use only such property as is necessary for a hunting cabin on the real estate hereinbefore described, and for such purpose only. Nothing herein contained shall bar Permitter from renting other parts of aforesaid real estate or using other parts, not needed by Permittee herein for a hunting cabin.

Permittee shall comply with all laws and administrative and commission orders of every kind and nature.

IN WITNESS WHEREOF we have hereunto set our hands and seals the day and year first above written.

In Presence of:

Sawyer County, Permitter

By

Members, Sawyer County Conservation Committee

Alvin Madson

Permittee

Unwritten Ownership Agreement

Protecting the original ownership was of paramount importance to the five original Jolly Boys. They all shared the fear that an "outsider" might create disharmony which could lead to the demise of the hunting camp. All had witnessed the failure of many other deer camps after resentment developed among camp members. They had all heard about camps that had folded when one or more members didn't pay their fair share of camp expenses or share responsibility for tasks such as dishwashing, cutting and bringing in firewood, etc. It was the only fair way to do things. They also knew that the younger members needed to handle the "grunt" work, with the older members pitching in to help when possible.

This was primarily an "understood" agreement. There was nothing in writing. If one of the members made the decision to leave the camp, the remaining owners would reimburse the departing member with only his net investment in the venture up to that point in time. The departing member could not sell his share of interest to anyone other than the remaining original Jolly Boys. They also agreed that if one of them should die, the ownership rights would not pass to the widow or the children. The last thing that any of them wanted was to find themselves in the position of dealing with the wife or children of the former camp owner.

They also agreed that no one would be allowed to invite a guest up to the camp without the prior approval of the others. This was their "blackball" system, and it, hopefully, would prevent any animosity between the Jolly Boys and eliminate the need to cope with a guest that someone else might dislike. This was to be a deer camp where everyone got along, and there was no place for anyone who couldn't hold their liquor or had bad manners. They further agreed that all deer taken during the hunt would be shared equally. At the end of the deer season, the deer would be butchered and the meat equally divided among all who wanted it. The coveted loins and back straps would be reserved for special Jolly Boy parties at the deer camp.

Construction of the Shack

The Jolly Boys had frequent meetings to plan how the hunting camp and shack would be constructed and equipped. The permit did not allow for a permanent foundation, so they decided to build on concrete block piers. Although the building would be new, they made a conscious decision at that time that they would call their camp "the shack," not "the cabin." Also in the plans, of course, was an outhouse. This would be large enough to contain a light plant so that electricity could be provided at night, rather than being dependent solely on gas or kerosene lamps. A friend of Merle's gave them a 1940s Kohler 1500-watt electric generator which looked like a small tractor engine. A crank was used to start it, like an old Model A Ford.

Ultimately, they chose a footprint about the size of a large garage, measuring 16 feet wide and 24 feet long. Building materials would be collected from salvaged lumber found in their own garages and backyards from discontinued projects or sources that might offer it free or at a low cost. Merle, who worked for Mrs. Sutliff in her lumber yards, would prove invaluable in obtaining greatly “discounted” lumber and materials that needed to be purchased.

The shack would be built facing north and south, with entry on the south side and the bunks on the north end. Large windows would be installed on the east and west sides of the shack to catch the early-morning and late-afternoon sun. The outhouse would be placed about 20 yards to the north of the shack, away from the main entrance for privacy, and the outhouse door would face to the east to catch the warmth of the rays from the rising sun.

Construction began in the summer of 1955, with the goal to be able to hunt out of it in the fall of that year. It was an enormous project. All of the material was hauled in with an old Jeep pick-up that Merle owned. Although the new site was only a half-mile from a major highway as the crow flies, the old logging road weaving through the woods leading to the camp was three-quarters of a mile long and frequently muddy, with many deep ruts. The Jeep, as well as any other mode of transportation, got stuck in the mudholes on a regular basis, and it took considerable effort to free the vehicle, often stuck down to its rocker panels. There were many work parties that summer. Construction was slow but steady and complicated by the many mosquitoes, deer flies, and wood ticks.

There weren’t many battery-operated power tools back then. Everything was cut by hand, every nail was driven by a hand-held hammer, and all of the lumber used consisted of tongue-and-grooved planks. Plywood and OSB board were unavailable or too expensive. The floor of the shack was constructed with tongue and grooved maple. They painted it gray because they wanted a floor they could scrub, and scrub they did. They almost always scrubbed their way out of the shack when they were leaving, using a mop, bucket, and Spic-and-Span. In the fall of the year, the floor would be repainted. Maintaining a clean floor was a cardinal rule of the Jolly Boys, a habit several of them had acquired during their military service. There was no insulation used in the construction of the shack, so the ceiling was left open to the rafters. Except for the bunk area, which had sheet rock, the walls were exposed wood, which proved to be the ideal place to hang Playboy centerfolds.

THE KITCHEN

Because the camp permit allowed the taking of down and dead timber for use in the camp, the Jolly Boys decided to use wood as their primary source of heat and cooking, as there was an abundance of yellow birch and maple in the area. One of the biggest "finds" the Jolly Boys managed to obtain for the shack was an old black Monarch wood-burning stove, complete with warming ovens and a warm-water reservoir. It had sat, no longer used, in the basement of the old First Lutheran Church, where the Jolly Boys were members, and the church was only too happy to trade the stove for the muscle power it took to remove it. Moving that old stove into the shack was an enormous undertaking. It served Blue Heaven well for many years and was the perfect solution for heating and cooking. It served up countless delicious meals and was a constant reminder to all that "old" was worth keeping and that there was irreplaceable value in craftsmanship. Next to the stove sat a small, used #1 fuel oil-burning stove which was used to provide minimal heat after the wood-burning stove had done its job and its fire had died out in the middle of the night.

An old wooden cupboard was found and placed inside the shack just to the left of the oil burner and wood cook stove. The inside was used as a pantry to stock the various staples needed to produce the meals for the hungry hunters. The top became their bar. The surface was Formica, and various liquor bottles sat there, neatly arranged and ready for cocktail hour which began sometimes early, sometimes late, but never later than 5 p.m. Bloody Marys were also mixed there, and everyone joined in for the mid-morning Bloody which was served prior to the huge lumberjack breakfast provided around noon of each day, when the hunters came back to warm themselves from the morning hunt. The Bloodys were served with a "snit" of beer from the beer keg which was constantly on tap during the deer season. Today that tradition endures, along with a new tradition that Bloody Marys are not consumed until someone has shot a deer and venison is hanging from the deer pole.

In the center of an eight-foot-long kitchen countertop the Jolly Boys installed an old single-basin porcelain sink. They washed the dishes in it, and it was strictly forbidden to use the sink for brushing one's teeth. That had to be done outside. The sink was located by the main entry, with a window over the sink so any deer could be spotted while a hunter was on KP duty. Pots and plans were stored on shelves below the countertop. Three large drawers were built, one to store silverware and cooking utensils; one for towels, dishcloths and hot-pads; and one for potato and onion storage. There were no cupboard doors; everything was open, neatly stacked, and visible for inspection. Everything in those cupboards was always kept sparkling clean.

Central to the shack was the table. It measured three feet wide and eight feet long, with a matching wood bench on one side and a number of mismatched chairs on the other side and at the two ends. It was, of course, a lumberjack-style table, and its functions included meals, card-playing and cutting up and wrapping venison. On a few occasions it became another bunk when all of the shack bunks were filled. The table was adjacent to two large windows, again to ensure that the hunters could watch for deer while they sat there.

BUNKS

One of the most important aspects of any serious and respectable hunting camp is the bunk area. In the tradition of the land in which they lived—lumberjack territory—the Jolly Boys thought hard about this design. They agreed they needed at least nine bunks: five for the founders and four for guests. The bunks would be located at the far end of the shack. Originally, there were eight single bunks and one double bunk to accommodate the possibility of a visit during the off-season by one of the wives. It was later determined that the double bunk wasn't really necessary and took up too much aisle space, so it was converted back into a single bunk. They managed to locate used old-fashioned springs and single mattresses. Three bunks were built against each of the two walls, and the other three bunks were placed between them in the center. The lower bunks were the coldest at night, whereas the upper bunks could be quite warm but were also quite high off the floor. The middle bunks were coveted, since they were easy to get in and out of and the temperature was more consistent.

Observing the Jolly Boys select their individual bunks was like reading the story of "The Three Bears." This one is too high and too warm. This one is too low and too cold. This middle one will be just right. My father selected the middle bunk on the left and was always extremely meticulous when making up his bunk. Frequently, he would haul his mattress out of the bunk area and put it on the lumberjack table to make it up at the beginning of the deer season. He would carefully put down a sheet to cover the mattress, followed by another sheet. He would then lay two quilts over the top to keep him warm at night. My father always slept in a long night shirt and would often put on a night cap to keep his bald head from getting cold. He always needed help putting back his made-up mattress.

Adder selected the center middle bunk for himself, as he felt that sleeping next to one of the outside walls would be too drafty in the early morning hours, when the inside of the shack frequently dropped to about 45 degrees. Adder also slept in a long flannel nightshirt and was equally fussy in the make-up of his bed. He insisted on using flannel sheets, flannel pillowcases, and wool blankets. Merle selected the middle bunk on the right side and was also meticulous about his bedding, using sheets and heavy wool quilts. He always slept in longjohns, as did Kenny and Howard. Howard slept below Merle and wasn't too fussy about his bedding. Neither was Kenny, who slept in the lower center bunk, choosing that bunk for the ease of getting in and out of it. Each of the Jolly Boys outfitted his bunk area with shelves to keep personal items close at hand. The bunks selected by the Jolly Boys were sacred territory, and when a Jolly Boy couldn't be in camp, his bunk was to remain untouched. Anyone violating this rule "would be sent packing down the trail."

The upper bunks were the hardest to climb into and out of, so they were given to the youngest hunters, who would have to crawl up and down from them using the other bunks as stepladders. The "still of the night" at the camp was frequently broken by the sounds of men leaving their bunks to go to the outhouse. On occasion, someone would fall out of his bunk and wake the rest of the entire camp. In what was more an effort to reduce noise from the late-night card-playing and storytelling, as opposed to providing a modicum of privacy, drapes were hung over the two entryways to the bunk area. The drapes also provided a barrier to keep the cigarette and cigar smoke from the sleeping area. The drapes did serve a big purpose when someone needed to take a sponge bath during the nine-day deer season. More on hygiene later.

Adder Madson clearing brush at the construction site—fall of 1955.

Merle Dunster and Marv Hanson squaring a corner of the shack. Note the concrete blocks used as posts for the foundation. This would prove to be problematic in years to come as the concrete blocks continually sank in the clay soil, requiring constant efforts to re-level the shack almost annually.

(L-R) John Hanson, Phillip Madson, Merle Dunster, John Dunster, Violet Hanson, Marv Hanson and Barbara Dunster enjoying a brief lunch break during the initial stages of construction.

Overview of the framed walls of the new hunting shack.

The Jolly Girls

The wives of the Jolly Boys included Violet (my mother), Gloria, Ellen, Elva and Puffin, and they named themselves the "Jolly Girls." High-spirited and good-hearted all, these ladies pitched in to assist their husbands in making the shack a success. They went through their kitchens and closets and gave over what must have been at that time, days shortly following World War II and still close to the Great Depression, items that meant something to them. They

The "Jolly Girls" (L-R) Ellen Madson, Gloria Dunster, Violet Hanson, Elva Nystrom and Norma "Puffin" Sugrue.

sacrificed pots and pans, tableware, cooking utensils, dishes and glassware, bedding, and towels. Even homemade quilts and coveted flannel sheets were provided by each household. Eventually, many of these items became antiques and collectibles, some rather valuable, but all treasured for the memories and sacrifices they represented in a time when husband and wife freely shared with each other. In many respects, the Jolly Girls came to enjoy the same bond developed by the Jolly Boys.

The Jolly Girls were aware from the beginning that this deer camp was for the exclusive use of their husbands. None of them ever complained when their husbands left for the nine-day deer season or when it was necessary for them to go up to the shack to handle all of the various construction projects and maintenance. The Jolly Girls knew that there would be many events at Blue Heaven in which they would be included, and all of them were glad for that.

My mother was an excellent seamstress and very talented with her sewing machine. She made the drapes to hang over the entryways to the bunk area. She also made the unique heavy-duty potholders for the cast-iron cookware used on the wood-burning stove. All of the Jolly Girls were superb cooks, and each of them took great pride in sending some of their delicacies up to the hunting shack for the Jolly Boys. One of these delicacies was Ellen's meatballs. She made them with ground beef, pork, and veal, and they were the size of tennis balls. They were always prepared a day or two before the opening of deer season. Adder would bring take them to camp, swimming in gravy, to be served on arrival at the shack so the Jolly Boys didn't have to be concerned about preparing the evening meal. Her meatballs were always served with sliced boiled potatoes and sliced boiled rutabaga with more than ample butter. It was comfort food at its best. When Ellen passed away, my mother volunteered to take over the chore of making her Norwegian meatballs for us. Although they were good, they were only the size of ping-pong balls. The tradition of the Friday night meatballs was passed on to me when my mother passed away, and I tweaked her recipe by adding crushed garlic. My two sons often competed in a meatball eating contest at the shack. There was never a clear winner or loser, but both consumed countless meatballs on that first Friday night in deer camp.

Norwegian Meatballs with Gravy

My parents both grew up eating meatballs, my sister and I grew up eating meatballs, and my two sons have inherited the taste and love for what I consider to be the best of the best of all comfort foods. Served with gravy, mashed or boiled potatoes, and rutabagas or a green vegetable, meatballs will keep everyone at the table until they can consume no more.

My mother's recipe was quite simple but somewhat bland. She would purchase about two pounds of finely ground chuck and a pound of ground pork and put it in a bowl. She would then add a teaspoon of salt, a quarter-teaspoon of pepper, two tablespoons of finely chopped onion, and a few shakes of Lowry's seasoned salt. She would then crack an egg and begin to combine the ingredients with her hands. While all of this was going on, she would have a half-cup of bread crumbs or one slice of dried bread soaking in a half-cup of milk. This would be combined in the bowl after the milk had soaked up all the bread crumbs or dried bread and then mixed in with the other ingredients. Once these were well blended, the real work would begin. She would start to roll the mixture into meatballs about the size of a ping-pong ball and place them in a skillet to fry in a little oil on low heat, turning them frequently so they would brown on all sides. Often, she would sit in a chair near the stove to watch over the progress of the slowly browning meatballs, lovingly turning them carefully so they wouldn't break up. Once the meatballs were browned to her liking, she would remove them from the skillet with a spoon, sprinkle two tablespoons of flour into the skillet, and shake the skillet to wet the flour. Two cups of cold water would be added, and she would stir the mixture constantly on low heat with a large fork until it thickened. The meatballs would then be put back into her gravy and slowly simmered in the skillet until it was time to serve dinner with the side dishes that she had carefully selected to complement the meatballs and gravy. Indeed, they were loved by all who sat at her table.

SHACK MEATBALLS

When I inherited the chore of making the meatballs and gravy for the first Friday evening at deer camp, I decided that although my mother's recipe was time-tested and great, I wanted to enhance it to kick the recipe up a few notches and bring it more in line with the other unforgettable menu items we serve at Blue Heaven. I immediately knew I could accomplish this by injecting minced garlic, horseradish, and additional minced onion into her recipe. This recipe will provide about eight normal servings.

Ingredients for the meatballs:

2 lbs. ground beef (80/20)

1 lb. ground pork

1 lb. ground veal (If veal is not available, use half ground beef and half ground pork)

1 cup unseasoned bread crumbs

2 eggs (beaten)

½ cup of milk

1 teaspoon salt

1 teaspoon Lawry's seasoned salt

1 teaspoon ground pepper

1 cup finely minced onion

1 tablespoon minced garlic

1 stick of margarine (for frying meatballs)

Combine all ingredients except for the margarine in a large bowl and mix completely, using your hands. Allow mixture to sit for about a half-hour. Roll meatballs in the palms of your hands to about the size of a golf ball and place the meatballs in a skillet with the melted margarine. Slowly brown the meatballs on all sides until cooked. If you prefer, you can bake the meatballs rather than fry them. Using a shallow roasting pan, bake the meatballs at 325-350 degrees for about an hour until oven-browned.

Prepare the gravy separately. The best way is right in the skillet using the drippings from frying the meatballs. Remove the meatballs and set them aside in a pan or bowl. Add three cups of cold water or milk to the skillet and turn the heat up to medium. Liberally salt and pepper the gravy to taste and add one tablespoon of horseradish. Using a small shaker or a small glass jar with a lid, mix flour or cornstarch with an equal amount of milk and shake well until blended. This will be used to thicken the gravy. When the gravy begins to simmer, slowly add the mixture a little at a time, stirring constantly with a whisk until the gravy reaches the desired thickness. Turn the heat down and place the meatballs in the gravy, allowing them to simmer slowly for at least an hour before serving. If you've decided to bake the meatballs rather than fry them, I would recommend using the recipe for "Shack Gravy" that you will find with the "Shack Steak" recipe further on in this book. To complement the meatballs even further, I would highly recommend that the jar of horseradish be placed on the table when dinner is served.

First Shack Log Entry

Much of the shack history can be told accurately because a shack log was kept, a tradition which continues to this day. There are three logs of recorded stories, told and written by many people who have both been a part of and known Blue Heaven.

A family outing at Blue Heaven in 1955. (L-R back row): Family friend Clifford Bergum, Jolly Girl Gloria Dunster (husband Merle was taking photo), Jolly Boy Adder Madson, Jolly Boy Marv Hanson, Ruby Bergum, Jolly Girl Violet Hanson and daughter Marilynn. Standing in front with the axe is the author, John Hanson, with Philip Madson peeking out directly behind, and Jay Peter Madson dressed up in his blue skiing parka.

The first shack log entry was written by my mother, Violet Hanson. Presumably, it was the first occasion of the Jolly Boys and their families at Blue Heaven. The entry reads:

> *"Family Housewarming held on Sunday, Nov. 13, 1955 – The following people were present:*
>
> *Marvin Hanson, Vi Hanson, Marilynn Hanson, John Hanson, Kenneth Sugrue, Dolly Sugrue, Pete Madson, Merle Dunster, Gloria, wife of Merle, John K. Dunster, Barbara L. Dunster.*
>
> *Boy! Can those Jolly Boys cook! Fabulous meal – pineappled ham, baked potatoes, cole slaw, peas, coffee and cookies. Pony keg too – Lots of fun! Broke camp 5:05 p.m."*

Deer Season 1955

Preparing for First Deer Season in New Shack

As deer season November 1955 approached, I watched my father's excitement grow as the days went by before the season opener. If we received a little snow his excitement would escalate, because there would be snow to track the deer and know where they were moving. The snow also lightened up the woods, making the deer easier to see. Our entire family loved venison, which was what the hunt was all about—the opportunity to bag a deer and provide meat for our table in the coming months.

Dad was going through many of the same preparations as in prior years, but this year it would be different. He now had his own hunting shack; the Jolly Boys had Blue Heaven. My father began accumulating his hunting gear in various parts of the house. His deer rifle had been carefully cleaned and was propped in its case safely in a corner in the bedroom. That way, no one could accidentally bump into it and screw up the sights. He had laid out his box of bullets, along with his deer knife, compass, license, hunting clothes, cigars, and other items "necessary" for the hunt, and he had a checklist for all things critical before leaving for the woods.

My mother took a very active role in this preparatory process. She was very supportive of the hunt and had taken great pains to ensure that an adequate amount of red cloth had been carefully sewn onto the old wool jacket that he wore while hunting. Blaze orange had not yet become a requirement for deer hunters. My mother, along with the other Jolly Boy wives, had also prepared cookies and other treats to send up to the new hunting shack for the deer season.

My father had a large white duffel bag in which he carefully packed all of his hunting gear. The duffel bag was from his service in the Navy, and he used it to transport his hunting gear to deer camp each year until he died. He would pack that bag until it couldn't hold one more thing—and then it would hold one more thing.

I was a young boy who wanted nothing more than to be able to go to Blue Heaven with my dad, who was aware of my disappointment that I could not go. I was simply too young to be around all of the high-powered rifles and the "colorful" language that would be spoken by the men while in camp. The Jolly Boys had decided early on that deer season would be a men-only event, as the shack was simply too small and crude to accommodate the opposite sex or young children. More to the point, it was their chance to get away from all of the pressures of daily life and to reconnect with nature and each other. They felt that anyone under the age of 14 simply was not old enough or mature enough to be included in their hunt. This was to become one of their many rules which all agreed upon and respected. It would be allowable for a boy 12 years old or older to come up to camp to hunt with his father for the day, and maybe even stay overnight if there was room, but he would not be allowed out in the woods without supervision. That was too risky for his safety and the safety of the other hunters in the woods. The possibility of young daughters accompanying their fathers to Blue Heaven was never discussed. The camp was for men only unless there was a family event.

In addition to each hunter preparing his own personal belongings to bring to camp for the hunt, there were other responsibilities assigned to get the camp ready for deer season. My father was in charge of preparing the list of supplies that would be needed for the season, Adder was to make certain that there would be an ample supply of water, and Howard was assigned the job of obtaining #1 fuel oil to operate the oil burner as well as gasoline to operate the light plant. Merle and Kenny were in charge of providing the transportation to haul all of the supplies and gear into camp, and of making certain that the Kohler light plant was functional for the season.

The supply list always occupied a considerable amount of my father's time prior to deer season. He spent hours at his desk with a cigar in his mouth, making out the supply list to try to make certain that adequate provisions would be on hand. The Jolly Boys had met previously in what they termed an "executive session," deciding on the menu for deer camp as well as who planned to be there and on what days people would be there to hunt. The list included paper products, staples, produce, dairy products, camp supplies, meat, multiple snack items, and, of course, an extensive list of beverages. Dad began shopping for the supplies weeks in advance, trying to purchase them when they were on sale and then bringing them home and carefully storing them in cardboard boxes to make it easier to transport the supplies into camp. Perishables weren't purchased until a day or two prior to the big day; my mother wouldn't allow her refrigerator to be held hostage.

Each year my father would modify his "Master Supply List," decreasing the supplies that he had purchased too much of and increasing the supplies that they had run short of as the season progressed. He had the procedure down almost to a science, and frequently at camp he would quip if we ran out of crackers, cereal, or other items, "I can never figure out how much you (expletive) are going to eat up here…." It was his standard line every deer season, and he would modify the master list accordingly, trying to be accurate as possible the following year.

Storage of all of these supplies at deer camp for the entire deer season was always a challenge. The camp had two discarded refrigerators, which sat out in the attached shanty to store meat and dairy products. These items had to be closely monitored, as neither refrigerator worked. If the weather was too warm, things would start to spoil, and if the weather was too cold, there was the danger that the eggs and other delicate items would freeze. Often, the delicate items had to be brought in and stored on the shack floor at night to keep them from freezing. At the beginning of the deer season, the cupboard would be overflowing with supplies, and it was always difficult to dig through it and locate things that were needed when they were needed. The paper products, such as toilet paper and paper towels, were placed on top of the dish cupboard or in other areas where space could be located and utilized.

Adder's job of overseeing the water supply was critical. The shack didn't have any running water, as the soil in that area was too rocky to drive a well in spite of several attempts. Adder would begin filling all of the water cans on the morning before the opening of the deer season to get them ready to be transported up to camp. The old milk cans we used had been obtained from Walt West at the Hayward Dairy and were extremely heavy. It often took two men to move them once they were filled. Abundant water was needed for cooking, dishwashing and having the occasional sponge bath while up at camp. The water was heated in kettles or large pots on top of the wood cook stove. The drinking water was brought in using empty one-gallon milk jugs, which were much easier to handle. All of the water was stored out in the attached shanty by the refrigerators. Frequently, the water would freeze out in the unheated shanty, so it wasn't unusual to find several water jugs thawing near the wood cook stove.

The other critical supply item was ice, which was needed to keep the perishables from spoiling if the deer season was warm. An ample supply of ice was also needed to chill the beverages and beer for the evening cocktail hours. This task was always the responsibility of everyone who had planned on being up at camp. Everyone was expected to make bags of ice cubes or freeze water in milk cartons to assure that there would be a sufficient supply for the entire deer season. The possibility of spending money to purchase ice was never a consideration by any of the Jolly Boys.

First Deer Season at Blue Heaven (1955)

A few days after the official housewarming on November 13, 1955, the shack log records the fact that Kenny, Adder, Marvin and Merle came up to get the shack ready for the first big day. It had been snowing all day, and the four inches of new snow on the ground obviously generated a considerable amount of excitement in the Jolly Boys.

The shack log entry of November 18, 1955 was recorded by Marvin who wrote:

> *"Well here we are!! Got here about six pm. Lots of snow - - about a foot or more. Howard & Dale, Merle, Marv - - Expect Pete Madson tonight. Had wieners and kraut, spuds, etc. Tapped a 'pony'. Real good, good, good - - This is living. Got a dollar apiece on the deer head horns for the first pair of n—ts. P.S. No nuts."*

The Jolly Boys had established a tradition that each hunter in their camp would place a dollar bill on the horns of an old deer head hanging in the bunk area. Merle had donated it after picking it up in a garage sale. The first hunter to shoot a buck during the season would claim the prize money. If no one killed a buck, the money would be placed in the shack fund at the end of the season. In 1955, deer weren't all that plentiful in northern Wisconsin. Based on data from that year, when there were 267,612 hunters and a "one buck, fork or larger" limit for each hunter, only 30,000 deer were harvested.

The shack log from the first season had only that one entry recorded. The log has grown in importance and length every year since then as traditions have evolved and memories have been created.

In the years that followed, Marvin would often speak about the difficulties of deer hunting in the deer seasons from that period. Naturally, everyone wanted to be up there to hunt, but because of their work schedules it was very difficult for the Jolly Boys to always be in attendance. Back then, all of them worked at least six days per week, and paid vacation time was very limited or non-existent. As a result, most of the Jolly Boys were unable to arrive at deer camp until late on the Friday night before the season opener. The lucky ones were able to get the first weekend of deer hunting off from their jobs or businesses, but it wasn't unusual to have the deer camp unoccupied during the work week. Mostly, the Jolly Boys were able to be there to hunt on the first weekend, Thanksgiving Day, and the last weekend of the nine-day gun deer season. Often, there were too few hunters up at camp to have a decent poker game, so they would play cribbage when there were only two or three hunters staying overnight in the shack. The beverage of choice back then was beer that was on tap from a "pony keg." The pony kegs of that time were about half the size of the current quarter barrels of beer. They had a cork on the top of the barrel, and there was always a contest among the Jolly Boys to see who could shove the tapping rod down through the cork and tighten the tapper before any of the beer escaped. It was a challenge to accomplish that task "without spilling a drop," and there were many friendly arguments between the Jolly Boys as to who was the most proficient.

The meals at deer camp back then were also simple fare, as money was tight and there frequently would be only a few hunters in camp to be fed. All of this would change as the economic situation of the Jolly Boys improved and their work schedules allowed more of them to be at camp more often.

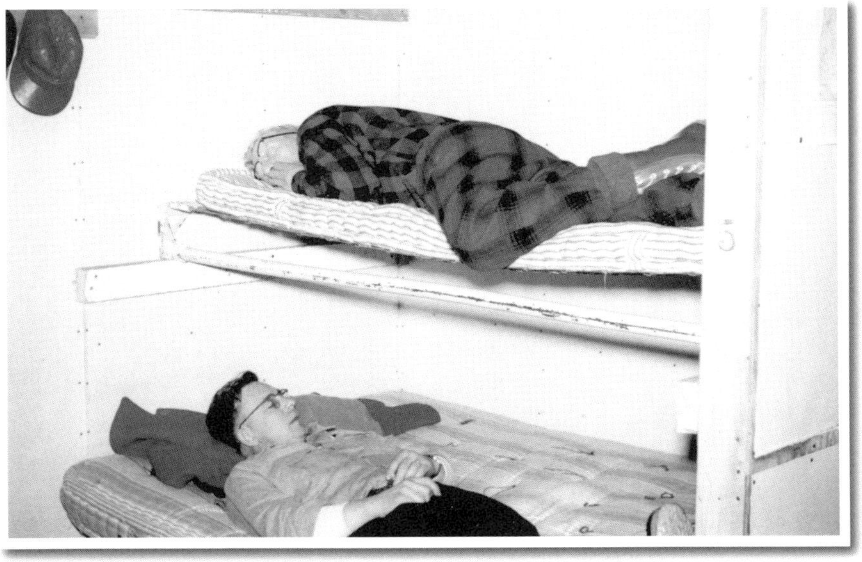

Jolly Boys Howard Nystrom in his lower bunk and Merle Dunster in his center bunk taking a quick nap at noon before returning to the woods to hunt. They must have arrived early on the first morning as their bunks are not yet made up.

Jolly Boys (L-R) Marv Hanson, Adder Madson and Ken Sugrue proudly displaying "the colors" in front of the buck pole during deer season.

It's For More Than Just Hunting

Blue Heaven was quickly becoming a family retreat for activities that went beyond deer hunting. The shack log reflects that on December 11, 1955, several of the Jolly Boys along with their families and other friends came up to the shack to hunt for Christmas trees. All had purchased one dollar permits from Sawyer County to harvest a Christmas tree off county property. It was a sunny Sunday afternoon outing with about a dozen in attendance. The shack was warmed with a fire in the old wood cook stove, and chili had been brought in for everyone to enjoy. There was beer for the adults and pop for the kids. It was a sunny winter day, with about three feet of snow blanketing the forest floor. The snow was almost waist-high in places, and it was difficult to walk through it. Violet wrote in the log:

> *"Merle, Gloria, Barbara and John walked six miles looking for a Christmas tree and found one scrawny one. These woods are good for other things, but not Christmas trees!"*

Although there were plentiful balsam and spruce trees in the area surrounding the new hunting shack, most were either too large to cut down or too deformed to adorn a living room.

The Jolly Boys were eager to show off their new hunting shack to all of their friends and began to invite guests to see their new hunting camp with parties that they hosted during the winter months. The shack log of those early years has numerous entries written by not only the Jolly Boys but also by many of their various Hayward friends whom they welcomed to their hunting shack for these events. Many of these friends became lifelong Blue Heaven aficionados, passing their own stories and memories on to the next generation. Based on the documentation found in the shack logs, one could easily fill this book with all of the activities, parties, and outings enjoyed by the Jolly Boys over the years. Let it suffice to say that these events were numerous.

Jolly Boy Merle Dunster hauling in supplies for a winter weekend retreat at Blue Heaven with one of the first Ski Doo snowmobiles in the Hayward area. (Circa 1960)

(L-R) Violet Hanson, Jolly Boy Marvin Hanson and Ellen Madson about to begin gliding through the snow into the shack for the weekend on cross-country skis.

DAD'S FAVORITE PLACE

I don't think anyone enjoyed his time at that hunting camp more than my father. It was his favorite place to be. He was always in the mood to make the trip up there and was ready to go at the drop of a hat. He was always willing to put together the supply list to make certain any event would be a success.

He meticulously maintained an inventory of all of the staples stored in the cupboard at camp and knew at a glance what supplies were needed. If anyone went there and used any of these supplies without informing him, they would feel my father's wrath when he found the supplies depleted.

God love my mother, she knew how much this hunting camp meant to my father and always encouraged his participation, doing whatever she could to assist him.

My father, like all the Jolly Boys, kept essential personal articles on hand in the small storage lockers assigned to each hunter. This was important because frequently one of them would be up there for a planned day trip and then decide to spend the night. There was always spare bedding available to accommodate the unplanned overnight guest, and one might even be able to find a spare unused toothbrush. So many of the events that occurred up there were impromptu, and that was a part of the fun of it all.

My parents couldn't afford expensive vacations in faraway places, nor did they have much desire to venture far from home. Their vacation destination of choice was a trip to Blue Heaven for a weekend or the entire week, if they could arrange enough time off work.

It cost them almost nothing for their retreats up there, and they would take ample food and beverages for their stay. They had this down to a science. My mother would even crack and place the eggs needed for breakfast into a small mason jar to help keep them cool in their ice chest and as a precaution so they wouldn't break. The same careful planning extended to the snacks they would bring, the ingredients for their meals, and the cocktails and other beverages that would be required. My father always enjoyed a martini or two before his evening dinner, so bringing the right number of olives was also important.

Both Mom and Dad loved to read and would bring a few good books with them in the event it rained and they couldn't be out in the woods hunting for partridge. My father would sit in his chair at the table, chin in his hands, with elbows planted firmly for support while he read. My mother was more innovative. She would make my father haul up a folding chaise lounge on these trips and would position it close to the wood cook stove to enjoy the warmth while she read and listened to the rain on the roof of the shack. They also always managed to sneak in an afternoon nap in the bunk area under one of the many soft quilts. Their cocktail hour would begin promptly at 5 p.m., along with a few snacks, and they often enjoyed a card game or two while dinner was cooking on or in the oven of the wood cook stove.

My parents learned that it was difficult to sneak away and get much time by themselves. Someone would invariably get wind of the fact that they were going to be up there and would either pay them "a surprise visit" or ask beforehand for permission to be included in the activities. The door was always open, and the more, the merrier! There always seemed to be more than enough to eat and drink, and those who came up and crashed the party would never show up empty-handed.

When bedtime came, my father would turn off the light plant and light the night candle in the event one of them would have to get up in the middle of the night. They would crawl into their bunks, and my father would fall asleep instantly. His snoring would break the silence and keep my mother awake. To counter his racket, she would use a small portable radio that had a cord with an ear-jack for private listening. My father was dead set against any type of electronics at the hunting shack. This included telephones, TVs, and radios. He wanted nothing to disrupt the tranquility of being in the woods. These and similar items were and always have been banned in the hunting camp. But my mother needed the device to help her fall asleep, and, although I think she knew that he knew that she was hiding her radio, he never said anything about it. To this day, I continue to bring my mother's radio up to the shack during deer season so I can get the weather forecast for the day. I will sit at the table, sipping on my coffee and waiting for the others to crawl out of their bunks, and get the news and weather from that beat-up old radio. As soon as the weather is announced, I turn up the radio and pull out the ear-jack to convert the radio to speaker so everyone can hear the weather forecast. As soon as it's concluded, I re-plug the ear-jack back in so I am the only one who can hear it. There are several hunters in our camp who are still amazed that I can turn on the radio at the precise moment that the weather forecast is being announced. I am keeping the ear-jack my secret.

The camp "night light" is a "plumbers' candle" placed within a candle holder, and the candle holder is then put inside a dishpan as an added safety precaution.

My father, Jolly Boy Marvin Hanson, sitting in his favorite spot at the lumberjack table, reading and enjoying a cigar on a fall day at the hunting shack. Without question, Blue Heaven was his favorite place to be. My dad and mother frequently went to Blue Heaven in the fall for a weekend to relax, hunt, read and enjoy the solitude of being deep in the woods away from it all.

Deer Seasons 1956 and 1957

The deer season of 1956 was very similar to the Jolly Boys' first season of being the proud owners of a hunting camp. Unfortunately, no deer were harvested. The snow was deep and no deer tracks were found in the immediate area. That year was still a buck-only season, but for the first time a spike buck was considered to be a legal buck. Although there were 284,645 licensed hunters in the Wisconsin woods that year, only 35,561 bucks were harvested. This did not deter the Jolly Boys. They all loved to be in the woods hunting, and they all also loved being a part of Blue Heaven. If no one shot a deer and they didn't have venison to dine on, there was always an alternate menu for their evening meals. They dined on baked ham, beef or pork roasts, or chicken and dumplings. Side dishes included shack baked potatoes and shack peas. A pony keg was constantly on tap, and they still had their array of evening snacks to go along with the poker games.

A "shack baked potato" is very much like a potato that has been baked in a campfire. The wood cook stove oven temperature is normally about 400 degrees when the firebox is full of wood, and a potato will bake in that temperature in about 45 minutes. The outside skin of the potato develops a thick, smoky- flavored crust. Served with ample butter, salt, and pepper, it is a treat one does not soon forget. Shack baked potatoes can also be duplicated at home in a conventional oven by cooking the potatoes at 425 degrees until the skin is crispy.

"Shack peas" are truly a Jolly Boy innovation served with the majority of the dinners at Blue Heaven and simple to prepare. They are made by taking three 15-ounce cans of LeSueur brand very young small sweet peas and placing them in a pot without draining the juice off the peas. A quarter-pound of butter is added, along with liberal salt and pepper, and then simmered for about an hour on the stove. A ladle is then used to dish the peas with their juice into small individual bowls. Shack peas are eaten with a spoon so one gets all the fabulous juice with the peas. They make an excellent side dish with a variety of menu items, and no one ever dares to refer to them as "green pus bags."

The old logging road leading into the camp continued to deteriorate. There were frequent episodes of getting stuck trying to get in or out of the hunting shack. Transportation was always a problem, and frequently a jeep stuck in the mud would be abandoned and dug out at a more opportune time. The road traversed several swampy areas, and the soil was mainly rock and clay-based. When the road was wet, it was a challenge to maneuver. Everyone knew that they would either have to make improvements

The final mud hole in the turnpike. This had to be navigated before arriving at the hunting shack which lies just beyond the mud hole at the top of the hill.

Bobby Hanson and Howard Nystrom working hard to remove a stuck jeep from the mud hole. The jeep frequently became hung up on frozen ruts in the logging road.

to the road or find a better mode of transportation to access the shack.

An entry in the log from that season is as follows: "We left two jeeps mired in the mud at the first bad spot in the turnpike. Ken and Marv abandoned the vehicles and they carried in the water, beer and grub."

Things were beginning to look brighter for the Jolly Boys during the deer season of 1957, as hunters were now allowed to bag one legal buck plus one "party deer." This was the first year that the party deer system was implemented, and everyone was very excited over the prospect of being able to get some "camp meat" for the table. To obtain a party deer permit, four hunters had to apply for the permit, and then one of the hunters would be able to shoot a deer of either sex to fill the tag. That year, 288,903 licensed hunters shot 67,870 deer, almost double the number from the previous year. The Jolly Boys had enough hunters to obtain two party permits. On opening day, Marvin shot a ten-point buck on the same ridge at which he had shot the twin bucks in 1954. Later that week, Adder killed a large doe, and his brother-in-law, Norm Schmickel, also filled one of the party tags.

They were pleased to finally have some venison to eat at camp, but the venison steaks cut from the hind quarters of the deer turned out to be unusually tough and chewy. My father decided that the venison round steaks needed to be tenderized to be edible, and he invented a new Swiss steak recipe for the shack that season, naming it—what else?—"shack steak." He cut the steaks into serving-sized pieces and used a large butcher knife to pound flour into the steaks to tenderize them. The steaks were then fried in hard shortening in the cast-iron fry pan until they were browned on both sides. They were then placed into a roaster and slow-cooked with a sauce that he had invented for the steak to simmer in. The new dish was out of this world and is now a regular at our hunting camp.

SHACK STEAK

Ingredients:

Venison steaks cut from the hind quarter of the deer

Flour

Salt & pepper

Crisco or any other brand of hard shortening for frying

3 6-oz. cans "Dawn Fresh mushroom steak sauce" (found either in the catsup or gravy areas on the grocery shelves.)

1 2-oz. package Lipton Onion dry soup mix

2 13.25-oz. cans mushroom stems & pieces

Horseradish

Water

Preparation:

Cut venison round steaks into ¾-inch serving-sized pieces and place on a cutting board. Sprinkle each steak on both sides with flour. Use a large butcher knife or meat tenderizer to pound the flour into the steaks on both sides to tenderize the meat. Salt and pepper the steaks, and place them into a frying pan with an ample amount of Crisco or other hard shortening. Fry steaks on both sides until they are brown and then place the steaks into a roaster. While the steaks are frying, use a separate pot to blend the three cans of Dawn Fresh mushroom steak sauce, two cans of drained mushrooms, and one one-ounce package of dry onion soup mix. Add about two cups of water to the mixture along with one tablespoon of horseradish and bring to a simmer.

Pour the sauce over the steaks and add enough water so that the steaks are covered. Use a tight-fitting lid to cover the roaster or cover the roaster with aluminum foil to make a tight seal. Bake the steak and sauce in the oven at about 325 to 350 degrees for about three hours. The sauce will initially be quite thin but will thicken during the cooking process from the flour on the steaks. The sauce can be thickened if needed by adding a little more flour or "Wondra" flour just before serving. The sauce makes excellent gravy for the baked or mashed potatoes that should be served with this dish, and "shack peas" are the perfect side dish. The leftover steak makes an excellent hot beef sandwich. This recipe also works great with beef round steak if venison is not available.

Everyone left hunting camp that year pleased with the successful deer season. The following spring the Jolly Boys began an effort to improve the logging road leading into the hunting shack. Bob Dunster, Merle's brother, had access to a front end-loader and a dump truck, and they were brought up to see if a foundation could be built in the seemingly bottomless mud holes. They spent the entire day loading and hauling fill into the swampy areas of the road. Initially it appeared that they were making some headway into improving the old logging trail into Blue Heaven. However, a very wet summer that year pretty much negated their efforts, and the road remained almost impassable.

• • •

FRYING VENISON STEAKS

One has to keep in mind that venison is a very lean meat and that it is almost impossible to know how tender the venison will be until some of it has been fried and tasted. Numerous factors, such as the age, sex, and diet of the deer, determine whether it will be tender or tough. It is also a very healthy meat, and, prepared properly, there is nothing tastier. “Shack Steak” is our preferred method of preparing venison steaks when we find that the meat is on the tough side. However, pan-frying the venison is by far our preferred cooking method when we feel it is relatively tender. Because venison is so lean, it is also very dry; there is very little marbilization of fat within the meat and therefore very little natural moisture to work with. My father always fried venison round steak (steaks cut off the hind quarter of the deer) and venison sirloins (back straps) until they were thoroughly cooked, taking too much moisture from the meat. The result was that the venison came out on the tough side, even though it had been relatively tender. We have learned through the years that the only way to fry venison steaks is medium-rare in order to preserve what little moisture the meat has to offer and to keep the steaks from becoming the consistency of shoe leather. Never overcook venison steaks!

TRADITIONAL VENISON FRY

Cut the venison steaks into serving pieces about one-half inch thick or slightly larger. The steaks need to be fried in a cast-iron fry pan. Cast iron will put a "sear" on the outside of the meat to lock in the moisture; using a non-stick frying pan will yield unacceptable results. Both the pan and the grease used to fry the steaks have to be hot. The steaks need to be fried quickly on medium-high heat to obtain the desired result.

Place the cast-iron fry pan on your stove on medium-high heat and allow it to heat for a minute or two. Put an ample amount of either Parkay or butter-flavored Crisco in the pan and allow it to melt. Do not use butter. Butter burns. As soon as the Parkay or Crisco becomes sizzling hot, add the room-temperature steaks to the fry pan. They should immediately start "frying." If not, your pan is not hot enough. Turn up the heat. While the steaks are frying, season them with Lawry's Seasoning Salt and pepper. Allow steaks to fry for about two minutes. Watch for blood starting to appear on the top side of the steaks and then flip them. Add more Parkay or Crisco if needed and allow the opposite side of the steaks to fry for another two minutes. Remove from the pan, serving them immediately while the steaks are still piping hot. (Hint: If the kitchen develops a slight blue haze while the steaks are frying, you know that the temperature of your frying pan is perfect!)

THE THOMPSON VENISON FRY

My youngest son, Ollie, has a very close friend named Danny

Thompson. His is a deer camp family, and they have developed a venison steak recipe to die for. Their secret is that they coat the lean venison steaks with flour and seasonings to lock in all the moisture of the meat while it is frying.

Use a one-gallon ziplock bag and put in two cups of all-purpose flour, about two tablespoons of Lawry's Seasoning Salt, and one tablespoon of black pepper. Mix contents of bag thoroughly by shaking the bag.

As before, cut the venison steaks into serving-size pieces about one-half inch thick or slightly larger. Place several of the steaks in the ziplock bag, shaking the steaks to coat them and then shaking off any excess coating as they are removed from the bag. For this recipe, it is acceptable to use a non-stick fry pan, if desired, as the steaks do not have to sear while they are being fried. They only need to be browned on both sides. As before, use ample Parkay or Crisco in the frying pan but fry the steaks on medium to medium-high heat, turning the steaks as soon as blood comes through on the top side of the meat. The coating on the meat locks in the moisture of the steak. We frequently have heated discussions in the evenings when we are about to have a vennie fry whether to have a traditional vennie fry or the Thompson vennie fry!

Deer Season 1958

On Saturday, November 15, 1958, the first day of the Wisconsin 16-day gun deer season for that year, Merle wrote in the shack log:

> *"A large crafty doe, and a lightning fast 8 point buck, attempted to charge by Merle at 100 yards, but he, also, with a lightning fast draw, dropped each with a single bullet. This skirmish was at 9:15 AM near "The Birch". They were both extremely difficult shots thru thick brush with both deer at high speed. A medal of merit is certainly due Merle for his skill used today…."*

This was an unusual deer season for the Jolly Boys, because the state had extended the deer season from nine to 16 days in northern Wisconsin. It was also an unusual year for weather, as the temperature climbed into the high fifties during the day. There was no snow, and the woods were very noisy. The Jolly Boys once again had two party tags, and the remaining party tag was filled with a doe the first Wednesday of the season. The Jolly Boys decided that a 16-day deer hunt was simply too long. As a result, they hunted for the first nine days of the 16-day season and didn't return to hunt for that final week. For the most part, the attempt at a 16-day season was a bust.

I was 14 years old that deer season. I remember that although I was allowed to hunt that year with a rifle, I stuck pretty close to my dad, learning the area around the hunting shack and trying to keep myself from getting lost. I was finally able to experience "shack life" and to spend a few nights in camp observing the poker game. I was amazed at how much fun my dad and the other Jolly Boys had up there. I quickly came to realize that deer hunting was about much more than the actual deer hunt. The biggest part of the hunt revolves around being in the woods and hunting out of a hunting shack. Getting the deer was almost secondary.

Deer Season 1959 – My First Hunt

Deer season 1959 will always be my season of endearment. It was the season I shot my first buck. I had spent the previous deer season hunting with my father, who was preparing me to hunt alone safely. I was allowed to carry a rifle, but it was a spare rifle borrowed from one of my uncles. The year 1959 was different. I was now allowed to hunt by myself, and I had my own new Winchester Model 94 .30-30. It was an excellent "brush gun" and known as "the gun that won the West." It was lightweight, accurate, and very dependable. I shot up a box of bullets test-firing my new Model 94, and I spent countless hours loading, unloading, and "dry-firing" it in order to become completely familiar with its open iron sights. I believed that I was totally proficient with its operation.

Fortunately, my upbringing was one that involved much time in the woods with my grandfather's Remington bolt action .22 that my grandmother had given me after my grandfather died shortly after my tenth birthday. My friends and I spent much of our free time hunting squirrels, rabbits, and other small game in the woods surrounding Hayward. I considered myself to be a deadly shot with the iron sights of that .22, prepared to move on to bigger game.

I was a freshman at Hayward High School. Like most northern Wisconsin schools, ours was understanding about the nine-day deer season and the tradition allowing students to hunt. School was still in session up to Thanksgiving, but a student was allowed to be absent if he made up his classes in advance.

I spent many sleepless nights in the weeks before opening weekend lying in bed, thinking about the approaching deer hunt. Visions of trophy bucks danced in my head, as did the gnawing worry that I would miss the buck at which I was shooting or encounter the dreaded "buck fever" that so many hunters spoke about. I had not yet shot a deer. As a matter of fact, I had not yet even shot at a deer. The deer herd was scarce in those days, and a hunter felt lucky just to jump a deer or see a "flag" running away from him in the woods. The time spent in the woods with my father in the seasons leading up to this year had been invaluable. I had learned the essentials of the deer hunt, and I had learned to do it safely. There were no required hunter-safety courses back then; one learned from the seasoned hunters. More importantly, my father had taught me about the woods surrounding our hunting camp and the many trails with which I needed to become familiar in order to avoid getting lost in the rugged terrain.

There was a very unfortunate complication in the first weekend of that season. My sister was scheduled to be married in St. Paul during the late afternoon of the first day of the hunt. My mother gave permission for my dad and me to go hunting on the opening day but said we had to be back home by noon to leave for St. Paul. There could be no excuses for a late departure.

The Friday night before the opening day of the season that year was similar to previous years up at the shack. Everyone was busy making their bunks and preparing their hunting gear so that they would be able to be in the woods at first light on the first day of the season. There was considerable conversation about where everyone was planning to be stationed on open morning, and each of the hunters had his favorite stand in which he would already be before first light. I was the youngest in the group, and my only plan was to be where no one else was hunting. Adder's wife, Ellen, had made a large pot of meatballs which were simmering on top of the old wood cook stove, along with a pot of boiled potatoes and a pot of rutabagas that would be our dinner that evening. Several of the hunters were gathered at the huge table playing poker, waiting for dinner to be served. I was only 15, too young to play poker with the older hunters, so my time was spent checking my hunting gear, making certain that I had all the critical supplies necessary to be carried into the woods on opening morning. Spare bullets, hunting knife, compass, matches, toilet paper, candy bars, hunting license, and all of the other essentials were strategically placed in my hunting coat which I kept out in the wood shed so it wouldn't smell of cigar smoke and other hunting camp odors.

Finally, at about 10 p.m., the poker game ended, dinner was served, and the dishes were washed and put away. Everyone prepared to crawl into his bunk to try to get a good night's sleep before the old wind-up alarm clock rang at 4:30 a.m. I crawled into my upper bunk between the soft, old quilts that my mother had sent with me and waited for everyone else to get settled in his bunk so the light plant could be turned off. Merle lit the oil burner to provide heat to the shack once the fire in the wood stove burned out, and he volunteered to go outside and hit the kill switch on the light plant. Everything went black once the light plant was shut down except for the dim light given off by a plumber's candle that was always lit and placed in the center of the table as a night light. The only sounds were the hissing of the old large teakettles on the wood stove, the crackling of the wood burning and snapping within the stove, and the tick-tick-tick of the old alarm clock that sat in the open cupboards with the dishes.

Although it was only about 10 degrees outside, the inside of the shack was warm, cozy, and quiet. Then the snoring began.... My father, who was only about three feet away from me, was the first to drift off into slumber and immediately began to emit sounds that rivaled the noise of an unmufflered chainsaw. Adder quickly joined the serenade. Merle and Howard joined the orchestra with a variety of their own harmonies, and the silence of the camp was gone. I then realized just how hot the upper bunks were. I soon had all of the covers thrown off and had two pillows covering my ears in a feeble attempt to block out the snoring.

It felt like the night lasted forever, and when the alarm clock rang at 4:30 a.m., I felt as if I hadn't slept at all.

I could smell the aroma of coffee perking on the gas hot plate that the Jolly Boys had installed for the purpose of making coffee immediately after getting out of bed. The fire in the wood cook stove had gone out sometime during the night. Getting the stove up to temperature to make coffee would be difficult and would delay the hunters from getting into the woods. I heard someone say, "What's the temperature outside?" There was a response from someone just returning from the outhouse: "It's about ten degrees, and the stars are still twinkling, but I can see some light in the east." I slid further down into my quilts, yearning to sleep until the shack warmed and the coffee was ready. Suddenly, my father shook my bunk violently and said in a loud voice, "Daylight in the swamp!" Reluctantly, I climbed down between the bunks and landed with a thud on the cold floor. The temperature in the shack was only 45 degrees. I hurriedly slid into my long underwear and put on my wool socks, knowing that it would soon be my turn to visit the cold outhouse. The inside of the shack was full of activity. Merle, the first one up, immediately started the light plant. He was now shaking the coals in the wood stove, trying to increase the fire to make the stove hot enough for the oven to make toast. The other hunters were busy getting dressed in their hunting clothes and double-checking their hunting gear. Cereal and milk were on the table, and the coffee cups were lined up.

Traditionally, the early morning breakfast at our hunting camp is always a simple affair. Everyone leaves the camp for the morning hunt and then returns to the shack around 11 a.m. for a large lumberjack breakfast at which stories of the morning hunt are shared and plans for the afternoon hunt developed. There are always several varieties of cereal on the table for the early morning breakfast, the most popular being raisin bran prepared with milk and extra sugar to provide needed energy for the hunters. Bread is toasted to a golden brown in the oven, heavily buttered, and served with peanut butter and strawberry jam.

The excitement of the hunt was in the air. All of the Jolly Boys, who had first choice of the prime deer stands, were declaring where they were going to be at first light on that opening morning. My father said he was walking up to sit near the "Little Rocks" which overlooked an extensive area of hardwoods on top of a large hill. Merle was going to his favorite stand called the "Birch." Adder was going a couple of hundred yards north of the shack to his stand that he called the "Chair," and Howard would be hunting the woods just east of the "Big Rock." My father told me to walk east on an old logging road that we called "Chicago Avenue" and head towards the Big Rock area to try to jump it toward one of the other hunters. The 1959 Wisconsin deer season was designated a one-legal-buck-per-hunter season, but four hunters could band together with a special permit to shoot a "party deer." We had one party-deer permit, and the Jolly Boys vowed that the party deer taken must be a large adult deer, not a yearling or smaller deer that wouldn't yield a lot of venison.

Everyone went outside to load their rifles and then headed for their deer stands to get settled by the time it was light enough to see down the sights of their rifles. I purposely waited on the road near the shack until I could see to shoot. The eastern sky was starting to turn pink, and although there were only a couple of inches of snow on the ground, it was enough to lighten up the woods and make it easier to see any movement. It was clear and crisp, and the wind was light and out of the northeast, making conditions ideal for my hunt. My father had taught me to always walk with the wind in my face when deer hunting. He told me that a deer's sense of smell was exceptional and that it was a wasted effort to hunt with the wind at my back. He had also taught me to walk slowly and watch each step, being careful not to step on a stick or anything else that might alert a deer to my presence. He taught me to be constantly aware of my surroundings and to look for any object that might be horizontal to the vertical trees.

By 6:45 a.m. I could hold my rifle up to my shoulder and align both sights, and I began my first hunt. There was enough snow on the ground to allow me to move silently down Chicago Avenue if I walked slowly and was careful with every step. I would pick out a point on the road, walk slowly to it, and then stand for a few moments, carefully examining the woods for any sign of movement or objects that appeared out of place before moving on. There weren't a lot of deer tracks in the area but there were a few. Most appeared old, but some appeared to be recent. Whenever I came across what appeared to be a fresh track, I grew more excited and alert, hoping that I was getting close to a deer. I was about halfway down Chicago Avenue and was stepping over a windfall on the trail when a partridge flew up from under the windfall between my legs. My rifle immediately went to my shoulder, and I had the hammer pulled back before I realized what had happened. It took several minutes for my heart to stop racing from the incident. The sun was starting to rise, and the woods were coming alive with activity. Red squirrels began their noisy chatter, chickadees were fluttering between the trees, and crows were flying overhead making gurgling sounds in their throats as they communicated with one another. Every so often, I could hear the sound of a rifle being discharged in the distance. None of the shots were close enough to be anyone from our camp, and I wondered if someone had gotten lucky and bagged his buck. I finally reached the end of Chicago Avenue, at the edge of a large tag alder swamp. Except for my encounter with the partridge flying up between my legs and seeing a few apparently fresh deer tracks, my hunt thus far hadn't yielded anything.

I was confronted with a decision as to where to go, now that I had finished my hunt down Chicago Avenue. I looked at my watch. It was shortly after 9 a.m., too early to start hunting back toward the shack, as I certainly didn't want to be the first one back. I was in a relatively unknown area of the woods, and although I didn't feel lost, I was somewhat uncertain as to where I was. I looked at my compass and decided to walk south, hoping to end up on Birch Street, an old logging road running parallel to Chicago Avenue. I figured the road was about a half-mile south of my present location.

The wind would be on my left shoulder, and I would follow the edge of the tag alder swamp, which showed evidence of established deer trails and a few fresh tracks. The Big Rock was located somewhere in this area between Chicago Avenue and Birch Street. Although I had been there on only one other occasion, I was hoping to find it again. I knew Howard was hunting east of there, and I could stand at the Big Rock for an hour or so, hoping Howard would kick a deer in my direction.

Shortly after I left Chicago Avenue to start my hunt towards the Big Rock area, I saw movement on the deer trail coming in my direction. My heart began to race. Was a deer coming in my direction? I quickly stepped off the deer trail, leaned against a large aspen tree, and put my rifle to my shoulder. If this was a deer, I was ready. I then realized that what I had seen was probably too small to be a deer. Right in front of me was a huge, fat wolverine walking on the deer trail directly towards me. He looked very mean, as if he owned the woods. I was trespassing, hunting in his area of the woods. I had never encountered a wolverine in the woods before but was very aware of their reputation for being aggressive and fearful of nothing. Thoughts raced through my mind. Do I shoot him or do I yield to him, hoping that he passes by me without an encounter? I pulled back the hammer of my rifle and decided to give him the opportunity to pass by me, but if he decided otherwise, I was ready for him. He was about six feet away when he veered off the trail and disappeared down into the protection of the tag alder swamp. I released the hammer from its cocked position, being both relieved and thankful that the two of us had made the right decision. I was also grateful that I would have an interesting tale to relate to the other hunters when I returned to the shack for breakfast later. It would be my first story for the Jolly Boys.

I continued my trek, walking slowly south on the deer trail. I could see that the deer trail was heading up into the hardwoods above the tag alder swamp. I looked at my watch, which told me that it was now almost 9:30 a.m. The sun was fully up and beaming through the trees. The warmth it provided felt good. Suddenly, I heard a muffled noise coming from my left and almost simultaneously saw a deer running perpendicular to me in my direction. The deer looked like a large doe, and I couldn't see any antlers. I quickly pulled back the hammer of my .30-30, put the rifle to my shoulder, took careful aim at the front shoulder of the deer, and pulled the trigger. The rifle discharged, but the deer was still running. I quickly ejected the spent shell and fired again. The deer was still running and was starting to turn away from me, heading up the hill into the hardwoods. Once again, I ejected the spent shell and fired a third shot. I saw the deer tumbling to the ground, sliding down into a small indentation on the forest floor. My heart was beating hard and I began to tremble. Had I been successful? Had I just killed my first deer? I rushed to the area where the deer had fallen and there it was, lying on the ground. As I approached it, I could see two twelve-inch spikes on the top of its head. I had just killed my first buck! Hail to the hunter! I was still trembling but managed to pull my deer knife from its shield so I could put my tag on the deer.

Suddenly the deer began to move and attempt to get up. Its head was weaving back and forth as if it were attempting to gore me. It was still alive, and I learned an important lesson that day: one never approaches a deer and assumes it's dead until the deer's eyes have glazed over. I quickly grabbed my rifle, which I had leaned against a tree, and shot the deer through the neck at close range. I sat down in the snow, hoping that my hands would stop shaking, and heard Howard's voice yelling at me as he was walking in my direction: "Are you the one doing all the shooting?"

I shouted out, "I just got my first buck!"

Howard found me, examined the deer, and then shook my hand to congratulate me on my success. He told me that he had jumped the deer in the tag alder swamp just a few minutes before I had started shooting. When I asked Howard where we were, he pointed to the "Big Rock" imbedded in the side of the hill, only about a hundred feet from where the deer had fallen. Howard told me that I had better get busy and "gut out" the deer. Embarrassed, I informed him that I didn't have a clue how to do that. I had read how to dress out a deer but had never seen it done. Howard took off his coat, took out his knife, and gave me a lesson on the proper way to dress a deer. We had just finished cleaning the deer when Merle appeared. He congratulated me on my success but then added that he was sorry he had chosen to sit on the Birch that morning rather than coming to the Big Rock to hunt after he had heard all the shooting coming from that direction.

Merle retrieved the deer heart and liver from the gut pile, placing them in a plastic bag to be brought back to the shack for pickled venison heart for our snack table and fried venison liver for a future breakfast. The three of us dragged the deer about 150 yards to Birch Street and walked back to the shack to get the jeep pickup to haul the deer back to hang on the buck pole. My father and Adder were already back at the shack, preparing pancakes and pork sausage with fried eggs for our lumberjack breakfast.

My father and I were able to leave camp and arrive home by noon to go to St. Paul to attend my sister's wedding. That entire day, my thoughts and heart were in the woods, reliving the hunt and my success at shooting my first buck. My father and I were back in deer camp by 10:00 p.m. that evening, ready to hunt again the next morning. Although I wanted to return to the Big Rock to hunt, Merle said that he was selecting it as his choice for a hunting stand and that because he was a Jolly Boy with the option to do so, I had to find other areas to hunt that season. Our camp shot two more deer that year: another small buck and a party-deer doe. Both were shot by Merle; both were shot at the Big Rock.

The season was declared a success, as 105,596 deer were harvested that season by 349,443 licensed hunters in Wisconsin. With five hunters, the Jolly Boys at Blue Heaven had harvested three deer. We had taken our proportional share.

I had shot my first buck at age 15. Four years later, I would shoot the biggest buck our hunting camp has ever taken and would also experience what hunters call "buck fever."

• • •

PICKLED VENISON HEART

This makes an excellent hors d'oeuvre during deer camp, and it's very simple to prepare. You don't often see it served outside of deer season.

Take one or more venison hearts and remove any excessive fat. Soak the heart(s) in cold salted water for 24 hours. Remove the heart(s) from the salt water and place them in a pot, covering the heart(s) with fresh water. Add about three tablespoons of pickling spices to the water, and then simmer the heart(s) on low heat for about an hour and a half. Remove the heart(s) and refrigerate until completely chilled. Slice the heart(s) thinly and serve on a saltine with a thinly- sliced piece of onion and salt and pepper.

FRIED VENISON LIVER

Fried venison liver has always been a favorite for breakfast at our deer camp. Very tasty, but not for the faint of heart.

Remove all excess membrane and fat from the venison liver(s). Place the liver(s) in cold salted water, refrigerating overnight. Remove the liver(s) from the salt water just prior to preparing, and then slice the liver into serving-sized pieces. Place the liver pieces into boiling water for about one minute to blanch them. Transfer the blanched liver pieces to a paper towel to remove excess moisture, and place the liver pieces in a bag with flour, shaking lightly to coat the pieces. Fry the venison liver pieces in Crisco or margarine in a cast-iron frying pan and serve with lots of crisply fried bacon, fried onions, fried potatoes, fried eggs, and plenty of ketchup.

The "Snacks"

The Jolly Boys were quickly earning a reputation for showing their guests how a hunting camp should be operated. Before dinner was served, it was a ritual that hors-d'oeuvres were put out on the kitchen counter for all to enjoy during cocktail hour while dinner was being prepared and the nightly poker game was afoot. Everyone was hungry after a day of hunting and needed something to tide them over until dinner had been cooked and served later in the evening. The snacks on display were a meal by themselves. They included items such as sardines; kipper snacks; bulk herring; various types of cheeses, including headcheese and the very smelly limburger cheese which was always stored in a glass jar; venison sausage; smoked fish; braunschweiger or liver sausage with a kosher dill slice; and such delicacies as "'tiger meat" or, in later years, my wife's paté. Everything was usually complemented with pieces of sliced onion or sliced rounds of kosher dill pickles and salt and pepper. Tubes of saltine crackers were opened and at the ready to place the snacks on.

The Jolly Boys of old always served "tiger meat" as one of their snacks. This was their variation of "steak tartare" and was a favorite of just about everyone back in the early years of the hunting camp. My father owned a grocery store which had a fresh meat counter. Just before leaving for a trip to Blue Heaven, he would take a few pounds of round steak, remove all excess fat from the edges, and put it through his meat grinder at least twice until it came out to the desired consistency. This could spoil easily and had to remain highly chilled. He took it up to the shack in the butcher paper in which he had wrapped it. When snack time arrived, he would unwrap the tiger meat and put it in a chilled bowl surrounded by ice. The "tiger meat" would be liberally spread on a saltine with a generous amount of chopped onion laid on top and then heavily salted and peppered. Everyone looked forward to "tiger meat,"but it could also generate some lower intestinal distress for those who overindulged in this treat. On occasion, the outhouse behind the shack was fairly busy. As the years passed, this hors-d'oeuvre was served less often and was eventually discontinued.

Another favorite snack at the shack is my wife's paté which ultimately replaced the "tiger meat" at our snack bar. Health concerns arose over the consumption of "tiger meat," and this evolved as a great substitute. We also proudly served this paté at a supper club that my wife and I operated in Eau Claire, Wisconsin.

KATHY'S PATÉ

(My wife was given this recipe in the 1970s by a man named Don Penberthy, with whom she worked in Madison, Wisconsin.)

Ingredients:

1 16-oz. tube chunk braunschweiger

1 1-oz. package dry onion soup mix

1 8-oz. container sour cream

1 tablespoon Worcestershire sauce

3 dashes Tabasco sauce

While allowing the braunschweiger to come to room temperature, combine onion soup mix, sour cream, Worcestershire sauce, and three dashes of Tabasco in a mixing bowl. Allow ingredients to sit for about 30 minutes to incorporate. Cut up the braunschweiger into small pieces and add to mixture. Mix and mash thoroughly with a fork or use a mixer if available. Chill and serve with saltine crackers. The flavor of this treat can really be enhanced by serving a thin round slice of kosher dill pickle or additional onion on top.

THE PROPER WAY TO EAT A SALTINE

We serve only one type of cracker with our multitude of snacks at our hunting camp. They are high-quality saltines and seem to be the perfect complement to any of the snacks that are being offered that evening.

One night I folded my poker hand and left the poker table to fix myself a couple of snacks and mix another drink. I took a saltine and placed a sardine on it along with a small bit of onion and a little salt. Just as I was about to devour it, Russ walked up behind me. I proudly showed him my creation, which I was just about to consume. I held it up to him to give him a better view of it and said, "Looks pretty good, doesn't it?"

Russ smiled and responded, "Yes, I think I'm also going to have a sardine, but you have your cracker upside down."

Totally confused by his comment, I responded, "Whaddya mean it's upside down?!"

Russ then proceeded to enlighten me in great detail on the proper way to eat a saltine. He explained that when the saltine cracker was being baked, salt was placed on the top portion of the cracker for flavoring. He said it was absolutely essential that when you put the cracker into your mouth, the salted side of the cracker needed to be down. That way, the salted side would enter your mouth and be next to your tongue so you could enjoy the full flavor of the saltine.

I examined my creation. My cracker was indeed upside down, and the salty side of the cracker would not have entered my mouth in the proper manner for me to obtain the full benefit of the salty side of the cracker. I took a new cracker and corrected my creation. To this day, I have never again allowed a cracker to enter my mouth in the incorrect manner and have since pointed out to a multitude of people that they were attempting to consume a saltine "upside down."

Trails, Roads, and Landmarks

After the Jolly Boys had been hunting in the area for about five years, they became familiar with the terrain and knew where they should position themselves to be successful at seeing and killing a deer.

I have read numerous books on deer hunting and have found that almost every camp has names for the various deer stands, walking trails, and logging roads that run through their hunting area. The Jolly Boys were no different, and they quickly began to name their deer stands and other landmarks so that when the day's hunt was concluded, each hunter could tell his story of where he had been that day and what he had seen. As I began to become familiar with the general area in which we hunted, I started to make maps. I transferred that information onto a large window shade along with a separate window shade showing the history of when a deer had been shot, the area where the deer was killed, and the name of the successful hunter. I was able to use the shack log to compile this information for the years before I was allowed to hunt up at Blue Heaven.

The area around the shack had a network of logging roads used by loggers back in the 1940s when they were harvesting basswood from the area. The main road into our camp ran from Highway 27 east past our hunting camp all the way to Nelson Lake, about two miles away. They named this road "Birch Street," as it passed by Merle's deer stand that he called "the Birch." Birch Street from Highway 27 to our hunting camp was always a mess, because it wound through many low-lying areas with swampland on either side of the road, and there were always mud holes. However, after Birch Street passed our camp, the road went into the hardwood hills and became a very decent road with only a few bad spots. The Birch was in the hardwood hills area, and Merle had built himself a platform between three yellow birch trees that overlooked a vast amount of hardwoods with a tag alder swamp about a hundred yards to the south of his stand. This area was always a hot spot for deer moving through the area, as they would stick close to the tag alder swamp to escape any danger they might encounter. Many deer have been shot from the Birch over the years, and although the three birch trees no longer are there, it is still a coveted deer stand for the hunters from our deer camp. Just below the Birch and next to the tag alder swamp was a logging road that was named "Snow Plow Road," which also ran east and west parallel to Birch Street. It was called that because when the Jolly Boys first started hunting in the area, there was a V-shaped wooden snowplow by the side of the road that had been abandoned by loggers. The old wooden snowplow has long ago rotted away, but we still refer to the road as Snow Plow Road.

The other main road in the area was named "Chicago Avenue." This road also ran east and west and was several hundred yards north of Birch Street. The road started by our hunting camp and continued east for about half a mile, terminating at the beginning of a large swamp. Chicago Avenue has several hot deer stands on or near this old logging road. The first stand was Adder's favorite that he nicknamed "the Chair." Adder built a platform between three basswood trees and put a chair on it. His stand was only about three hundred yards northeast of the hunting shack and overlooked a cedar swamp running through a small ravine down to a tag alder swamp. It was a great stand, and many deer have been taken from or near this stand, which is now only a memory, the platform and Adder's chair having long ago become the victim of the elements.

About 100 yards east of the Chair just off Chicago Avenue is an area that is called "the Ravine." The Ravine is high on a hardwood hill overlooking a tag alder swamp to the north. There is a cedar swamp next to Chicago Avenue which allows for natural deer movement between these two areas. Another hundred yards brings one to a stand called "the Crotch." At one time, a large basswood stood next to Chicago Avenue with a huge crotch in the lower part of the tree in which a hunter could sit to view the surrounding hardwoods and a small creek which ran through towards a swamp. This was a natural draw for deer passing through the area.

About 50 yards east of the Crotch is a stand we call "the End of Chicago Avenue," which terminates near a tag alder swamp. In recent years, this area has yielded numerous deer for the hunter who has the patience to sit in a tree stand at the end of Chicago Avenue in the early morning hours or at dusk, when the deer are moving.

Branching off Chicago Avenue and running north is a road that has been named "North Lane." This road is almost overgrown and has diminished to a faint trail, but it runs through a stand of very thick tag alders and hardwoods that is definitely "big buck" country. Just before North Lane turns to the east, there is a stand that we named "the Can" because loggers had left a five-gallon gas can hanging on a tree. Some of the bigger bucks in recent years have been shot in this area from tree stands because the area is a blend of tag alders, popples, and pine trees.

Running east from the shack is a road we call "Little Rock Road." This road branches off from Chicago Avenue and then runs parallel between Chicago Avenue and Birch Street for almost a mile. It goes up a huge hill containing two sizeable rocks which have been inappropriately named "the Little Rocks." The view from this stand is amazing. If you continue east on Little Rock Road, you will go through an evergreen swamp and up to another large rock called "the Big Rock." The Big Rock is actually smaller than the Little Rocks, but nobody has bothered to change the names of these landmarks over the past 50 years. Until recently due to nearby logging operations, the Big Rock was probably the most successful deer stand in our area.

About 100 yards south of the Big Rock is a stand that we named "the Horse Barn." There was a small abandoned one-horse barn used by the loggers years ago, and the elements have finally rotted the barn into the leaves. The barn stood next to Chicago Avenue in a ravine with a small creek running through the area. At one time, it was a very good deer stand, just like the Big Rock, but logging has changed the terrain in the area, and deer seldom pass through anymore.

On the west side of the shack is a road we refer to as "the Upper Swamp Road," and on the south side of the shack there is an extension of that road we call "the Lower Swamp Road." The Upper Swamp Road runs north up to a point near the Chair and then terminates in the wet area of a cedar swamp. It's an excellent hunt going through this area. The Lower Swamp Road goes south for a half-mile down to the Jolly Fisherman Road, which is a main roadway to cabins on Nelson Lake. Logging in this area in recent years has left the area with thick underbrush, and it's very difficult to hunt, due to limited visibility.

If all of these names, terrains, and descriptions leave you befuddled, that's okay. You have to hunt there for years before you see the big picture.

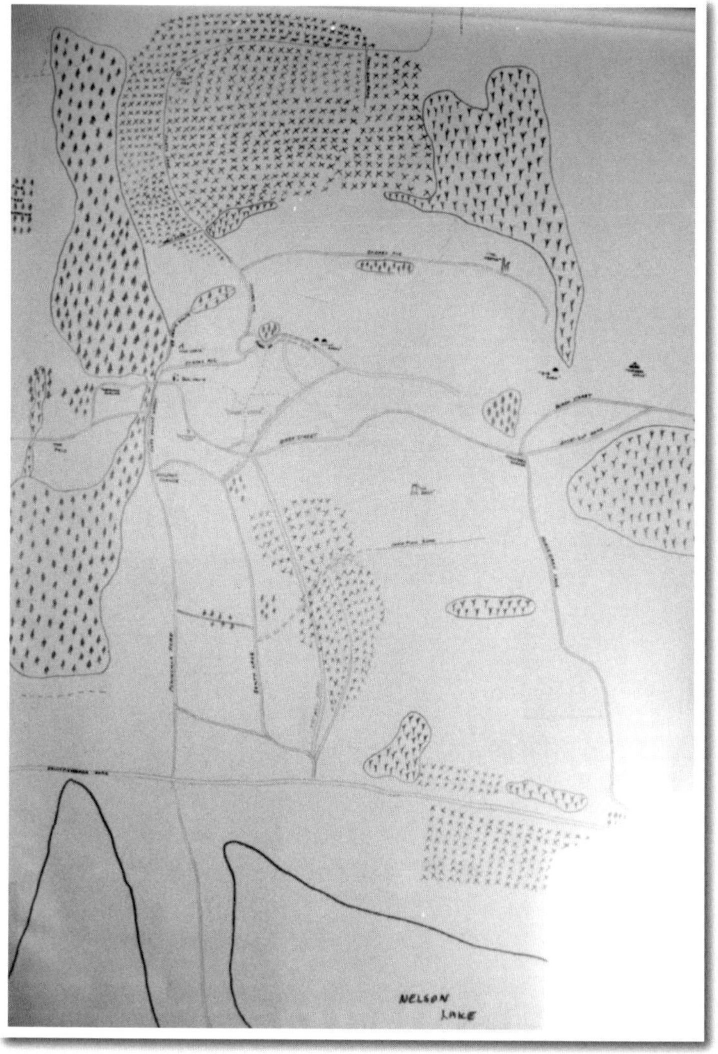

"The Map" is a map drawn on a window shade showing all roads, logging roads, trails and landmarks within a one-mile radius of the hunting camp. It was drawn on a shade so it could be retracted when not in use, but is frequently pulled down during the deer season to plan for the deer hunt or to show others where someone plans to spend the day hunting. It is also used for a hunter to show where he had been in the area and where he saw deer or deer sign.

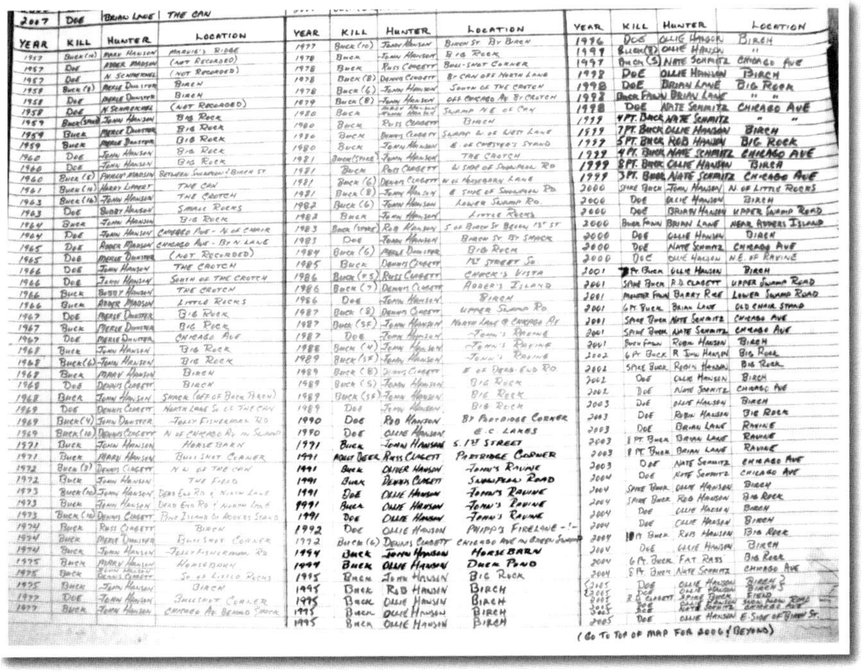

YEAR	KILL	HUNTER	LOCATION
2007	Doe	Brian Lane	The Can
1957	Buck (10)	Mary Hanson	Marvie's Ridge
1957	Doe	Roger Madson	(Not Recorded)
1957	Doe	N. Schmeckel	(Not Recorded)
1958	Buck (8)	Merle Dunster	Birch
1958	Doe	Merle Dunster	Birch
1958	Doe	N. Schmeckel	(Not Recorded)
1959	Buck (Spike)	John Hanson	Big Rock
1959	Buck	Merle Dunster	Big Rock
1959	Buck	Merle Dunster	Big Rock
1960	Doe	John Hanson	Big Rock
1960	Doe	John Hanson	Big Rock
1960	Buck (5)	Phillip Madson	Between Swampfeld & Birch St
1961	Buck (10)	Harry Lippert	The Can
1963	Buck (16)	John Hanson	The Crotch
1963	Doe	Bobby Hanson	Small Rocks
1964	Buck	John Hanson	Big Rock
1964	Doe	John Hanson	Chicago Ave - N of Chair
1965	Doe	Roger Madson	Chicago Ave - By N. Lane
1965	Doe	Merle Dunster	(Not Recorded)
1966	Doe	John Hanson	The Crotch
1966	Doe	John Hanson	South of The Crotch
1966	Buck	Bobby Hanson	The Crotch
1966	Buck	Roger Madson	Little Rocks
1967	Doe	Merle Dunster	Big Rock
1967	Buck	Merle Dunster	Big Rock
1967	Doe	Merle Dunster	Chicago Ave
1968	Buck	John Hanson	Big Rock
1968	Buck (6)	John Hanson	Big Rock
1968	Buck	Mary Hanson	Birch
1968	Doe	Dennis Clagett	Birch
1968	Buck	John Hanson	Shack (Off of Birch [illegible])
1969	Doe	Dennis Clagett	North Lane So. of The Can
1969	Buck (4)	John Dunster	Jolly Fisherman Rd
1969	Buck (10)	Dennis Clagett	N of Chicago Av in Swamp
1971	Buck	John Hanson	Horse Barn
1971	Buck	Mary Hanson	Bullshot Corner
1972	Buck (8)	Dennis Clagett	N W of The Can
1972	Buck	John Hanson	The Field
1973	Buck (10)	John Hanson	Dead End Rd & North Lane
1973	Buck	John Hanson	Dead End Rd & North Lane
1973	Buck (10)	Dennis Clagett	Pine Island or Rogers Stand
1974	Buck	Russ Clagett	Birch
1974	Buck	Merle Dunster	Bullshot Corner
1974	Buck	John Hanson	Jolly Fisherman Rd
1975	Buck	Mary Hanson	Horsebarn
1975	Buck	John Hanson / Dennis Clagett	So. of Little Rocks
1975	Buck	John Hanson	Birch
1977	Doe	John Hanson	Bullshot Corner
1977	Buck	John Hanson	Chicago Av Behind Shack

YEAR	KILL	HUNTER	LOCATION
1977	Buck (10)	John Hanson	Birch St. By Birch
1978	Buck	John Hanson	Big Rock
1978	Buck	Russ Clagett	Bull-Shot Corner
1978	Buck (8)	Dennis Clagett	By Can off North Lane
1978	Buck (6)	John Hanson	South of The Crotch
1979	Buck (8)	John Hanson	Off Chicago Av By Crotch
1980	Buck	[illegible]	Swamp N.E. of Can
1980	Buck	Russ Clagett	Birch
1980	Buck	Dennis Clagett	Swamp W. of West Lane
1980	Buck	John Hanson	E. of Chester's Stand
1981	Buck (Spike)	John Hanson	The Crotch
1981	Buck	Russ Clagett	W. Side of Swampfeld Rd
1981	Buck (6)	Dennis Clagett	W. of Horsebarn Lane
1981	Buck (8)	John Hanson	E. Side of Swampfeld Rd
1982	Buck (6)	John Hanson	Lower Swamp Rd.
1982	Buck	John Hanson	Little Rocks
1983	Buck (Spike)	Rob Hanson	S. of Birch St Below 1st St
1983	Doe	John Hanson	Birch St. By Shack
1984	Buck (6)	Merle Dunster	Big Rock
1985	Buck	Dennis Clagett	1st Street So.
1986	Buck (+5)	Russ Clagett	Chuck's Vista
1986	Buck (7)	Dennis Clagett	Roger's Island
1986	Doe	John Hanson	Birch
1987	Buck (8)	Dennis Clagett	Upper Swamp Rd
1987	Buck (SF)	John Hanson	North Lane @ Chicago Av
1987	Doe	John Hanson	John's Ravine
1988	Buck (4)	John Hanson	John's Ravine
1989	Buck (SF)	John Hanson	John's Ravine
1989	Buck (8)	Dennis Clagett	E. of Dead-End Rd.
1989	Buck (5)	John Hanson	Big Rock
1989	Buck (SF)	John Hanson	Big Rock
1989	Doe	John Hanson	Big Rock
1990	Doe	Rob Hanson	By Partridge Corner
1990	Doe	Ollie Hanson	E.C. Lakes
1991	Buck	John Hanson	S. 1st Street
1991	Adult Deer	Russ Clagett	Partridge Corner
1991	Buck	Oliver Hanson	John's Ravine
1991	Buck	Dennis Clagett	Swampfeld Road
1991	Doe	Ollie Hanson	John's Ravine
1991	Buck	Ollie Hanson	John's Ravine
1991	Doe	Ollie Hanson	John's Ravine
1992	Doe	Ollie Hanson	Phipp's Firelane -!-
1992	Buck (6)	Dennis Clagett	Chicago Ave in Green Swamp
1994	Buck	John Hanson	Horsebarn
1994	Buck	Ollie Hanson	Duck Pond
1995	Buck	John Hanson	Big Rock
1995	Buck	Rob Hanson	Birch
1995	Buck	Ollie Hanson	Birch
1995	Buck	Ollie Hanson	Birch
1995	Buck	Ollie Hanson	Birch

YEAR	KILL	HUNTER	LOCATION
1996	Doe	Ollie Hanson	Birch
1997	Buck (8)	Ollie Hanson	"
1997	Buck (5)	Nate Schmitz	Chicago Ave
1998	Doe	Ollie Hanson	Birch
1998	Doe	Brian Lane	Big Rock
1998	Buck Fawn	Brian Lane	" "
1998	Doe	Nate Schmitz	Chicago Ave
1999	4 Pt. Buck	Nate Schmitz	" "
1999	7 Pt. Buck	Ollie Hanson	Birch
1999	5 Pt. Buck	Rob Hanson	Big Rock
1999	4 Pt. Buck	Nate Schmitz	Chicago Ave
1999	8 Pt. Buck	Ollie Hanson	Birch
1999	3 Pt. Buck	Nate Schmitz	Chicago Ave
2000	Spike Buck	John Hanson	N. of Little Rocks
2000	Doe	Ollie Hanson	Birch
2000	Doe	Brian Hanson	Upper Swamp Road
2000	Buck Fawn	Brian Lane	Near Rogers Island
2000	Doe	Ollie Hanson	Birch
2000	Doe	Nate Schmitz	Chicago Ave
2000	Doe	Ollie Hanson	N.E. of Ravine
2001	[illegible] Pt. Buck	Ollie Hanson	Birch
2001	Spike Buck	R.D. Clagett	Upper Swamp Road
2001	Monster Fawn	Barry Rae	Lower Swamp Road
2001	6 Pt. Buck	Brian Lane	Old Chair Stand
2001	Spike Buck	Nate Schmitz	Chicago Ave
2001	Spike Buck	Nate Schmitz	Chicago Ave
2001	Buck Fawn	Robin Hanson	Birch
2002	6 Pt Buck	R John Hanson	Big Rock
2002	Spike Buck	Robin Hanson	Big Rock
2002	Doe	Ollie Hanson	Birch
2002	Doe	Nate Schmitz	Chicago Ave
2003	Doe	Ollie Hanson	Birch
2003	Doe	Robin Hanson	Big Rock
2003	Doe	Brian Lane	Ravine
2003	8 Pt. Buck	Brian Lane	Ravine
2003	8 Pt. Buck	Brian Lane	Ravine
2003	Doe	Nate Schmitz	Chicago Ave
2004	Doe	Nate Schmitz	Chicago Ave
2004	Spike Buck	Ollie Hanson	Birch
2004	Spike Buck	Rob Hanson	Big Rock
2004	Doe	Ollie Hanson	Birch
2004	Doe	Ollie Hanson	Birch
2004	10 Pt. Buck	Rob Hanson	Big Rock
2004	Doe	Ollie Hanson	Birch
2004	6 Pt. Buck	Fat Rass	Big Rock
2004	8 Pt. Buck	Nate Schmitz	Chicago Ave
2005	Doe	Ollie Hanson	Birch
2005	Doe	Ollie Hanson	Birch
2005	R.D. Clagett	Spike Buck	Field
2005	Doe	Ollie Hanson	[illegible]
2005	Doe	Nate Schmitz	Chicago Ave
2005	Doe	Ollie Hanson	E. Side of Birch St.

(Go To Top of Map For 2006 & Beyond)

Another pull-down shade hanging next to "The Map" provides the official record of deer harvested in the area in prior years by the hunters from Blue Heaven. The records start in 1957 and go through the current year providing information about the year the deer was taken, the type of deer shot, the hunter who enjoyed the success, and the location of the kill. The shade coordinates and condenses the information provided in the official "Shack Log" which records information from each season.

The Early 1960s: Porcupines and V & MM

Sometime during the early spring of 1960, I overheard my father talking in a very hushed voice to Merle on the phone. My mother was standing close by, and I knew something was wrong. I learned that Howard and Elva had separated. All of the Jolly Boys and their wives were devastated over this news. No one knew where Howard was, having disappeared without contacting any of the other Jolly Boys. Merle and my father decided that they should walk into the hunting shack to see if Howard was staying up there. To their relief, there was no sign that he had been there. They later learned that he had moved to the Twin Cities area and that the marriage between Howard and Elva was in the process of being dissolved. It was as if there had been a death in the family. They had been a big part of the Blue Heaven family, and this development would leave a big void in the group. We never saw Howard again. Several years later we found out that he had remarried and passed away a few years after that from a heart attack.

Merle and his wife Gloria walked into Blue Heaven on a routine inspection trip in September of 1960. Although the shack had survived the summer in many ways, a porcupine had forced his way into the outhouse and chewed the heck out of the wood on the interior. Porkies love salt and will chew on anything and everything that has been touched by the human hand. The outhouse obviously was attractive to the porky, and it had done quite a bit of damage. Porkies were plentiful in the area and could be easily seen high in the tops of basswood trees. They were starting to become a problem for us. The light plant also failed to start, and Merle had to make arrangements to take it into town to accomplish repairs.

Although the Jolly Boys made occasional inspection trips into the shack during the summer months, the shack was seldom used for any recreational activities, as it was too difficult to cope because of the wood ticks, mosquitoes, and deer flies. The grass around the shack grew waist-high during the summer months and had to be cut down in the fall when the weather cooled and the growing season ended. All of the Jolly Boys and their families looked forward to the first weekend in October. The weather was cool enough to build a fire in the wood-burning stove to cook, the bugs had pretty much disappeared, and the fall colors were in their full glory. Both my mother and Merle's daughter, Barbara, had their birthdays on October 1st, and everyone would look forward to going into the shack to celebrate the birthdays and open up and clean the shack for the upcoming hunting season. The men would bring their shotguns and walk the many roads and trails in the area, hunting for partridge and checking out recent signs of deer for the upcoming deer season. Many would choose to stay overnight. The standard Saturday evening dinner would consist of a huge beef pot roast with carrots, onions, and potatoes cooked in the old wood stove, or a large pork roast with summer squash and mashed potatoes. Of course, there was always plenty of delicious gravy. My mother always referred to the areas around the shack at this time of the year as "the golden land." I too use that term with my wife, Kathy, when we drive through all of the woods and trails that I favor in the fall, due to all the abundant gold maple trees that surround the shack in their full color during that time of the year. Against a deep-blue fall sky when the sun is high, there is nothing more beautiful. Even today the roads are marked as the "Fall Color Tour." I can still hear my mother singing, "Autumn leaves are now falling, see them tumbling down… Autumn leaves are now falling, red yellow and brown…."

There was not much said in the shack log about the 1960 deer season. It reflected the fact that I shot two does at the big rock and that Phillip Madson, Adder's youngest son, shot a five-point buck in the balsam pines just south of Birch Street. We called Phillip "Phip." He was about 14 at that time and was hunting close to his father when he saw a deer running at full speed and managed to shoot it after several shots. I had been hunting near an area we call Bullshot Corner, which was about a hundred yards west. I heard several shots and knew that Adder and Phip were hunting over in that area. I decided to head in that direction to see if they needed any help. It was a beautiful day with mild winter temperatures, and the snow on the ground was knee-high. It was slow going, but as I got closer to the area where I had heard all the shooting, I could see that there were three hunters standing in close proximity to each other, apparently arguing. As I got closer, I recognized Adder and Phip but not the other hunter, who had his back towards me. As I approached, I could hear the stranger arguing in a loud voice that Phip had shot the stranger's deer, which he had allegedly just shot and wounded minutes before the deer came up on Phip. Phip wasn't saying much, but Adder was making his son's argument known that the deer might have been slightly wounded but was running through the woods at express-train speed when shot by Phip. It was obvious that they were at a stalemate as to who had the right to that deer, neither willing to concede the kill. The woods were so quiet with all the snow that the stranger had not heard me approach from his rear. Adder and Phip had seen me coming, and I stopped about twenty feet behind the stranger. Eventually, the stranger must have felt my presence. He suddenly turned and was startled to see me standing there with my .30-30 cradled in my arms, with my hand in the lever and my finger on the trigger. The stranger must have realized that this was an argument he wasn't going to win with the three of us surrounding him, and he was upset but walked away. I watched him closely until he disappeared from our view. It was my first and only confrontation with a hunter as to who had the right to a wounded deer. I hoped that it would never happen again. I realized that day that a hunter wanted to claim "his" deer. It was an instinct that I had learned from my father and one that goes to the heart of not just "the kill" but the pride of "the hunt."

The following deer season in 1961 was pretty much of a loss for the hunters at Blue Heaven. The weather was too warm, there was no snow, and the woods were very dry and noisy. We all suspected that most of the deer had left our area in an attempt to find water, as even the swamps were dried out. My father and I, along with Merle and his Navy friend Bob Larsen, Adder and his two sons, and Merle's son "JK", had spent the entire season hunting without seeing any deer. On the last Saturday of the nine-day season, Kenny invited his new son-in-law, Harry Lippert, to the shack to hunt with us and see what our hunting camp looked like. Harry had never been in the area before. He walked north of the shack about a half-mile near the area we call "the Can," which is surrounded by tag alder swamps and thick underbrush. He came across an old grey ten-point buck and downed the deer with one bullet. He dragged the deer back to the shack by himself, and we were all were there to inspect his trophy. As the deer was lying there, we all witnessed dozens of wood ticks crawling off it. It was an unusual sight to see all of these insects abandoning their host, and we all wondered why this deer had so many wood ticks attached to it. That evening, Harry took his deer, wood ticks and all, back home to skin it out and cut it up, since the weather was too warm to allow it to hang for very long.

The following summer, Merle made a summer inspection trip into the shack in July and found that a porcupine had eaten through the wire mesh on our vent window and had entered the shack. He killed it with a pitchfork that was available in the shanty. The porky had done considerable damage, having chewed on the backs of all the chairs, the entry door, and everything in the shack that had been touched by the human hand which had the slightest taste of salt. The porky had taken up residence for quite some time, and the place was full of its droppings. The shack was a mess, and the following weekend everyone came up to witness the damage and clean things up. From that point forth, war was declared on porcupines in the area and the order was issued to kill any seen within a mile of the shack. This went against the mentality of the Jolly Boys, because we all believed that nothing should be killed unless the meat would be consumed. It was also common knowledge that a porky was a very slow animal and that a lost hunter could actually catch one by hand and use it as a food source if he became lost in the woods. Nonetheless, if a porky was sighted in the area of the shack, it was eliminated.

Porcupines were not the only destructive problem that the Jolly Boys had to address that year. They had always considered themselves to be fortunate that the shack had escaped any vandalism or theft. It was far from the nearest highway, and the road leading into the shack was almost impassable. Therefore, it was very unusual to see anyone coming back into that area, unless it was someone whom we knew and who knew where the shack was located. Over the years, I had invited several of my friends up to the shack to hunt partridge or squirrels, and many of them knew the location of the shack and the hidden door key. One fall evening, unknown to me or anyone else, several of my seventeen-year-old friends made an uninvited trip into the shack with several cases of beer. Their intent was to simply use the shack to party and drink and to leave it undisturbed. They let themselves in using the key to the door and spent several hours drinking beer. They all became quite intoxicated, and one of the uninvited guests accidentally broke a dish or a glass on the floor. As is typical with a group of young boys, everyone joined in on the carnage. By the time they were done, they had broken all of the dishes, all of the windows, and anything else that could be shattered. Merle had made a routine inspection trip to the shack on the following day and discovered the vandalism. He immediately contacted the Sheriff, and a deputy was dispatched to document the damage and investigate the incident. While Merle and the deputy were still there, the guilt had gotten the better of one of my friends, who returned to the scene of the crime to inspect what they had done the night before. It was obvious to Merle and the deputy that this individual had had some involvement, and after a short period of questioning, he confessed to the crime and named his accomplices. The parents of my four friends were contacted, and all came to the shack to clean up the mess, repair the damage, and offer restitution for the items that weren't reparable. The Jolly Boys had a meeting and decided not to file charges, as they believed that the parents would be able to impose suitable punishment. As a result, my four friends involved in the incident were all kicked off the football team, and most of them were grounded for the rest of their natural lives by their parents. To this day, it is a regrettable memory but one that enforces the sanctity of the camp: Thou shalt honor it.

The Evening Songfests

I find it difficult to describe the love of singing that the Jolly Boys and their friends always showed at Blue Heaven. The singing sessions would begin when the poker game was concluding and final preparations were being made to serve the evening meal.

The lengthy happy hours leading up to the songfest played no minor role in putting everyone in the mood to sing. The shack sing-a-long was usually initiated by Merle, who would jump up from the poker game and start passing out songbooks to everyone. The songs they sang were primarily from their generation of the 1940s—songs well-known to all of them, rooted in memories of the World War II era. Classic hits like *“Irene, Goodnight, Irene,” “Paper Doll,” ”Only You,” “Peg O’ My Heart,” “You Made Me Love You,” “It Had To Be You,” “I’m Looking Over A Four-Leaf Clover,” “I’ll Get By,”* and *“If I Loved You”* were just some of the standards. Of course, the Jolly Boys’ favorite song was *“My Blue Heaven.”*

The lyrics of many popular songs had been mimeographed by one of the Jolly Boys and put into booklet form so everyone could sing along without missing a word. Everyone knew the melody, and no one had a problem with volume.

Some of the songs begged for harmony—songs by groups such as the Mills Brothers and the Platters. Valiant attempts were made, not always with "harmony."

My father was an experienced bass from years of playing bass instruments in a dance band. He also had practical experience singing bass in the church choir. Kenny Sugrue had a mellow voice that was admired by all, and he had a special gift of soft vibrato in his voice. He was usually the one who would take the lead in starting the song in proper pitch. Merle would always sing the lead part and did so with a great deal of volume and enthusiasm. Frequently, the veins in his forehead and throat would stand out as he attempted to drown out the others in the group. The other participants would either follow my father trying to sing the bass part or sing lead along with Kenny. When the rare moment came that everyone actually produced a decent-sounding chord, the group would stop and revisit that part of the song. They sometimes surprised themselves.

Radios and mechanical devices for the reproduction of music at our hunting camp were forbidden. We always made our own music and entertainment, a tradition which has carried on to this day. The songfest tradition carried on into all the gatherings at the hunting shack. Whenever there were people at the shack, there was music.

After my father passed away in 1994, much of that music at Blue Heaven died with him. The generation that followed wasn't familiar with the songs in the songbooks. But late at night when the lights are out and the bunks are full, I can almost hear the Jolly Boys and all of their friends still singing the old songs.

(L-R) Marv Hanson's brother Clifford, Jolly Boys Adder Madson and Merle Dunster along with Russ Clagett doing a little quartetting.

Jolly Boy Merle Dunster playing the tonette while "Camp No-Hunt" members (L-R) Carl Nordquist, Carl Bensen, Dane Nelson, Harold Gobler and Bruce McGill participate in the nightly sing-a-long.

KAHN AND DEPINTO

Sez

DON'T JUST SIT THERE ON YOUR FANNY
SING ALONG WITH *JIM & MANNY*

COMPLIMENTS OF

POINT O PINES RESORT

WHEN IRISH EYES ARE SMILING

When Irish eyes are smiling
Sure it's like a morn in Spring
In the lilt of Irish laughter
You can hear the angels sing.
When Irish hearts are happy,
All the world seems bright and gay,
And when Irish eyes are smiling,
Sure, they steal your heart away.

MY WILD IRISH ROSE

My Wild Irish Rose. the sweetest flower that grows;
You may search everywhere, but none can compare
With my wild Irish Rose.
My wild Irish Rose, the sweetest flower that grows,
And some day for my sake, she will let me take
The bloom from my wild Irish Rose.

DOWN BY THE OLD MILL STREAM

Down by the old mill stream — where I first met you,
With your eyes of blue — dressed in gingham, too —
It was there I knew, that you loved me true;
You were sixteen — my village queen —
By the old mill stream.

PRETTY BABY

Ev'rybody loves a baby that's why I'm in love with you
Pretty Baby, Pretty Baby;
And I'd like to be your sister, brother, dad and mother too
Pretty Baby, Pretty Baby.
Won't you come and let me rock you in my cradle of love
And we'll cuddle all the time,
Oh! I want a lovin' baby and it might as well be you
Pretty Baby of mine
Pretty Baby of mine.

YES SIR, THAT'S MY BABY

Yes, Sir, That's my baby
No, Sir, Don't mean maybe
Yes, Sir, That's my baby now.
Yes, Ma'am we've decided
No, Ma'am, we won't hide it.
Yes, Ma'am, you're invited now
By the way, By the way
When we reach the preacher I'll say
Yes, Sir, That's my baby
No, Sir, don't mean maybe,
Yes, Sir, That's my baby now.

MARGIE

Margie, I'm always thinking of you, Margie,
I'll tell the world I love you; don't forget your promise to me,
I have bought a home and ring and ev'rything,
For Margie, you've been my inspiration,
Days are never blue; after all is said and done,
There is really only one, Oh! Margie, Margie, it's you.

ANGRY

Dearie, please don't be angry
Cause I was only teasin' you
I wouldn't even, even think of leavin'
Honey 'cause I love you true.
Just because I took a look at somebody else,
That's no reason, you should put poor me on a shelf.
Dearie, please don't be angry
'Cause I was only teasin' you.

WHEN YOU WORE A TULIP

When you wore a tulip, a big yellow tulip
And I wore a big red rose.
When you caressed me
'Twas then heaven blessed me
Such a blessing no one knows.
You made life cheery
When you called me dearie
'Twas down where the blue grass grows,
Your lips were sweeter than julep
When you wore a tulip,
And I wore a big red rose.

REMEMBER WHERE YOU GOT IT

SMILES

There are smiles that make us happy,
There are smiles that make us blue,
There are smiles that steal away the tear drops,
As the sunbeams steal away the dew,
There are smiles that have a tender meaning,
That the eyes of love alone may see,
And the smiles that fill my life with sunshine,
Are the smiles that you gave to me.

PEG O' MY HEART

Peg O' my heart, I love you
We'll never part, I love you
I always knew, it would be you
Since I heard your lilting laughter
It's your Irish heart I'm after,
Peg O' my heart your glances
Makes my heart say "how's chances?"
Come be my own,
Come make your home in my heart.

I DON'T KNOW WHY

I don't know why, I love you like I do,
I don't know why, I just do.
I don't know why, you thrill me like you do,
I don't know why, you just do.
You never seem to want my romancin'
The only time you hold me is when we're dancin'
I don't know why, I love you like I do,
I don't know why, I just do.

IN THE GOOD OLD SUMMER TIME
(Modern Version)

In the good old summer time,
In the good old summer time,
Strollin' thro' the shady lanes,
With your baby mine;
You hold her hand and she holds yours,
And that's a very good sign
That she's your tootsey wootsey
In the good old summer time.

HARVEST MOON

Shine on, shine on harvest moon up in the sky,
I ain't had no lovin' since
January, February, June or July.
Snow time ain't no time
To sit outdoors and spoon.
Shine on, shine on harvest moon
For me and my gal.

EASTER PARADE

In your Easter Bonnet, with all the frills upon it
You'll be the grandest lady in the Easter Parade,
I'll be all in clover and when they look you over
I'll be the proudest fellow in the Easter Parade.
On the Avenue, Park Avenue
The photographers will snap us
And you'll find that you're in the Rotogravure
I could write a sonnet about your Easter Bonnet
And of the girl I'm taking to
The Easter Parade.

DAISY BELL—(Bicycle Built For Two)

Daisy, Daisy, give me your answer do,
I'm half crazy all for the love of you.
It won't be a stylish marriage; I can't afford a carriage,
But you'll look sweet upon a seat of a bicycle built for two.

MOONLIGHT AND ROSES

Moonlight and roses bring wonderful mem'ries of you,
My heart reposes in beautiful thoughts so true.
June light discloses love's olden dreams sparkling anew;
Moonlight and roses bring mem'ries of you.

MY BLUE HEAVEN

When whippoorwills call, and evening is nigh,
I hurry to my blue heaven.
You turn to the right, a little white light
Will lead you to my blue heaven.
I see a smiling face, a fire place, a cozy room
A little nest that's nestled where the roses bloom
Just Molly and me, and baby makes three
We're happy in my blue heaven.

WHO'S SORRY NOW

Who's sorry now? Who's sorry now?
Whose heart is achin' for breakin' each vow?
Who's sad and blue? Who's cryin' too?
Just like I cried over you.
Right to the end, just like a friend,
I tried to warn you somehow.
You had your way, now you must pay
I'm glad that you're sorry now.

IN THE GOOD OLD SUMMERTIME

In the good old summer time,
In the good old summer time,
Strolling thro' the shady lanes,
With your baby mine;
You hold her hand and she holds yours,
And that's a very good sign,
That she's your tootsey wootsey in
The good old summer time.

IT'S A SIN TO TELL A LIE

Be sure it's true, when you say "I love you"
It's a sin to tell a lie.
Millions of hearts have been broken
Just because these words were spoken
I love you, yes I do, I love you
If you break my heart I'll die
So be sure it's true, when you say "I love you"
It's a sin to tell a lie.

SHOW ME THE WAY TO GO HOME

Show me the way to go home,
I'm tired and I want to go to bed.
I had a little drink about an hour ago,
And it went right to my head.
Wherever I may roam, on land, or sea or foam,
You'll always hear me singing this song,
Show me the way to go home.

I'M FOREVER BLOWING BUBBLES

I'm forever blowing bubbles
Pretty bubbles in the air
They fly so high nearly reach the sky
Then like my dreams they fade and die.
Fortune's always hiding
I've looked everywhere
I'm forever blowing bubbles
Pretty bubbles in the air.

(L-R) Marv Hanson, Adder Madson, Marv's brother Kenneth and Merle Dunster showing everyone how it's done.

(L-R) Bobby Hanson, Dick Gillis, Kenny Sugrue, Ken Hanson, Bruce McGill, Father Bob Hanson and Vern Inhoff working on the art of group harmonizing.

(L-R) Jolly Boys Marv Hanson and Merle Dunster leading everyone in song while working through the song sheets.

(L-R) Jolly Boys Merle Dunster, Marv Hanson and Adder Madson practice new songs late at night by the light of the Aladdin lamp.

1963–The Monster Buck

In the fall of 1963, the Jolly Boys decided that it was time to replace the Kohler light plant that Merle's friend Adrian Faase had donated to Blue Heaven. The Kohler light plant was the ideal solution to generate electricity for the shack, but the Jolly Boys were growing impatient with its mechanical problems. Many times the light plant wouldn't start, and several times it had quit operating and couldn't be restarted. The light plant had been operating in the same small building that served as our outhouse, and although it provided some heat for the hunters when using the outhouse, it was too difficult to work on in such a small space. Merle, Adder and his oldest son Peter, and I drove to the shack early in September of that year and poured a concrete slab for the replacement. On top of the slab, we poured a concrete stand to bolt down the engine. We found an old outhouse that was still in good condition and attached this building to the slab. It was hard work mixing all of the concrete by hand in a wheelbarrow, but things went smoothly. A couple of weeks later, we returned to install the replacement light plant, which was identical to the original. The old light plant was saved for spare parts, as this model had been discontinued by the

Our seemingly ageless 1500-watt Kohler light plant sitting atop and bolted to a concrete pedestal. Probably manufactured sometime in the 1940s, it still is today our dependable source of electrical power to light the interior of Blue Heaven. With a little "TLC" and frequent oil changes, it has been kept running like a watch and is much quieter than current generators.

manufacturer and replacement parts were very difficult to obtain. Late that evening, we lifted the 500-pound light plant onto its concrete pedestal, getting it installed and operating. It purred like a kitten, and the lights were one hundred percent brighter. The project was declared a success.

The Kohler light plant is a 4-cylinder, 4-stroke, gas-operated engine with a 2-inch bore and a 3-inch stroke. It generates 1500 watts of DC power at 115 volts and operates at 1000 rpm. The putt-putt-putt sound that it generates is a soothing background effect that is comforting to all who have spent any time up at the hunting shack. Over the years we have purchased two additional similar light plants strictly for the purpose of supplying spare parts to keep the current light plant functional. The old Kohler light plant remains our main source of electrical power to this day.

There are only four short entries in the shack log from the 1963 deer season. The reason is obvious.

11/22/63 - Marv & Bob H. came out in PM with supplies. Merle at about 8. John H. and Phip after BB game. ***Pres. J. F. Kennedy assassinated.***

11/23/63 – John H. got his buck – 12 (?) pointer.

11/25/63 - John K. Dunster got 1st shot at buck. Merle, John H., and John K. tracked for 4 hours & came out near Seeley fire lane. Didn't find.

11/26/63 - Ken S. out for delicious ribs & kraut. Delightful poker game.

Although the shack log didn't record much detail of that deer season, I still recall all of the events of that week.

I was nineteen and had taken a semester off from college to work at a woodworking factory in Hayward to earn tuition money so I could return to school for the second semester. It was Friday, November 22, 1963. I was packed and eagerly awaiting the factory whistle when the factory shut down at 3:30 that afternoon. Shortly after our lunch break, I saw one of my co-workers racing between the different employees in our area of the factory, yelling something at them, but I couldn't hear him because of the dozens of saws that were in operation. Finally, he arrived at my work station. His face was pale, and he yelled in my ear, "President Kennedy was shot and killed in Dallas this afternoon!" Several of my co-workers had already shut their machines off and were heading to the parking lot to listen to their car radios to try to get more information. I did the same. Available information was limited, but it was soon becoming evident that President Kennedy had been assassinated and that the assassin had been captured right after the incident. I, along with everyone else, had the same thoughts. Was it connected with the Russians? Were we going to war? Under the circumstances, was deer season going to happen this year or should we cancel it and remain home close to our families?

The plant manager gathered everyone together, and told us that he was letting us all go home early that afternoon. I used one of the office phones and called my father. He had heard the news and was very upset. However, he sounded relatively calm and assured me that we would still be heading for deer camp. We would take portable radios up with us to keep in touch with the outside world and would return home if necessary. The excitement of the impending hunt was greatly overshadowed by the uncertainties of that day's events. Our usual Friday night pre-hunt excitement was replaced by a somber atmosphere, and the majority of that evening was spent by us and the entire nation listening to radio and television for any new developments regarding what the future had in store for us and our country. When we crawled into our bunks that evening, everyone's thoughts were more on the day's events than the opening day of deer season, which was only a few hours away.

The shack alarm clock sounded at 5 the next morning. Our portable radio was immediately turned on for any news, and we were all relieved to learn that the assassination was apparently the work of one lunatic and that we weren't going to war with the Russians or anyone else. The Vice-President had been sworn in as our new President, and it seemed that the FBI had everything under control. We could now concentrate on the hunt without worrying about having to return home.

In addition to my dad and me, our hunting group that year included my dad's younger brother Bobby, Adder and his two sons Peter and Phillip, along with Merle and Howard. There were eight of us, so we would have good hunter saturation in the woods on opening morning, and we were all optimistic that one of us would shoot and kill a deer. Everyone announced where they planned to sit on that first morning except me. I wasn't much good at "sitting." My plan was to slowly hunt while walking east on Chicago Avenue until I reached a landmark that we called "the Crotch," which was a low crotch in a huge basswood tree that one could sit in overlooking a creek bed that ran north through Chicago Avenue. I planned to stand there for a bit and then move on when I tired of looking at the same piece of woods. I was too impatient to stand or sit in one location for too long. I always had to see what was going on over the next hill. I had developed my own style of hunting. I loaded my Winchester Model 94 .30-30 with eight bullets. Seven were inserted in the tube of the rifle, and one was locked in the chamber. I was ready for action and left the warmth of the hunting shack at 6:30 that morning, just as it was getting light enough to see the front and rear sights of my rifle.

I walked about 50 yards through the woods and arrived on Chicago Avenue, an old, not yet overgrown logging road built sometime back in the 1940s, and began my hunt. There was only a trace of snow on the ground, so even walking on this road was noisy, with the still-frozen leaves covering the road. I took every step slowly and carefully, trying not to step on a branch or give any indication that I was moving through the woods. I would move slowly for about 25 or 30 yards, and then stop for a minute or two to look and listen to see if there was any movement in the woods ahead of me, on my sides, or to my rear. My father had taught me well in this regard, pointing out that trees grew vertically, and that one needed to look for anything that was horizontal or looked out of place. I was also looking for any disturbance of the ground covering which might indicate that there were deer in the area. The skies were clear, so the woods were getting brighter by the minute and the sun would soon be filtering through the trees. The sun would be warm enough to melt the little bit of snow on the ground, so it would be a difficult day for anyone to track a wounded deer.

I continued my hunting method, traveling east on Chicago Avenue for about half an hour. Slow walk…stop…look…listen. I had reached a point where the Crotch was almost in view. There were a few deer tracks in the area, but none appeared to be that fresh. I could hear frequent shots being fired in the area, but none were close enough to be anyone from our hunting party. To my right was an evergreen swamp with a heavily-mossed floor and a combination of cedar and hemlock trees. It was a beautiful area, and I had walked through it many times in past deer seasons, always finding numerous deer beds. The trees were mature, and one could look through the swamp to higher ground beyond. The swamp was alive with early morning activity. Chickadees were fluttering between the trees. Red squirrels were running around underneath the trees, chasing each other and giving their shrill warning cries to let everyone know that a stranger was approaching the area. All of a sudden, I saw a flash of movement. My rifle went immediately to my shoulder, but by the time I pulled my hammer back, I realized that it was only a partridge. I had spooked it, and it was flying away from me to make its escape. I lowered my rifle, released the hammer, and continued my slow walk past the swamp. The Crotch came into my view, and the snow on the ground showed that there had been considerable deer activity in that area overnight. I was starting to feel very optimistic that I might see a deer.

I'm not certain to this day whether I heard the deer and then saw it or saw the deer and then heard it. About 70 or 80 yards to my right, I saw a huge deer running perpendicular to me at almost full speed down the hill through the basswoods. Obviously, it had been kicked out by another hunter, and the deer was heading to the tag alder swamp just to the north of the Crotch, seeking safety. I instinctively pulled the hammer back on my .30-30, raised the rifle to my shoulder, took careful aim at the animal's left front shoulder, and fired. The bark from my rifle broke the tranquil silence of the swamp, and all of the animals within went on full alert. I quickly ejected the spent shell, saw the magnificent antlers on the deer shining in the morning sun, aimed, and fired again. I ejected and fired five more times, and on my eighth shot, I saw the deer stumble and crash to the forest floor. My heart was racing and my hands were trembling. My rifle was empty. I threw off my gloves and fumbled through my jacket pocket. I pulled out five more bullets and shoved them into my .30-30. The deer was down but was still making a valiant attempt to get back up and run to safety. He was able to raise his hind legs but was unable to raise himself up on his front legs. I fired again, and again, and again, and again. He finally was down. I ran over to where the magnificent animal was lying, taking his final breaths. I raised my rifle and fired my remaining bullet into his thick neck. There was no further movement. I sat down on a windfall near him, marveling at him and the deed that I had just done. My hands were still trembling, but I managed to reload my rifle with a few additional bullets just in case he miraculously recovered and attempted to escape. The green swamp, now to the back of me, quickly quieted down and returned to its peaceful and tranquil state.

After a few moments, I collected myself, stood up, leaned my rifle against a nearby tree, and grabbed the buck by its antlers. I thought I had shot a ten-point buck, but there were twelve large points, with two smaller points on each side of the rack. It was a legal sixteen-point buck! His coat was grey, and his teeth were worn way down, indicating that he was an old, wise, swamp buck that had escaped death over the course of numerous deer seasons due to his ability to elude the wrath of a hunter's rifle. He was a trophy, and he was my trophy.

I took off my jacket and field-dressed him. I wiped my hands on several red handkerchiefs that I had with me and began the forced march back to the shack. On my arrival, the shack was empty and it was only about a quarter after eight. I walked over to the old deer head with the buck dollars on it, removed them, and put them in my pocket. I didn't want to risk having my trophy discovered in the woods by another hunter, so I started the Coot and drove back to the scene of the kill. On my way, I picked up Peter, and the two of us loaded the deer into the back of the Coot. The deer was heavy, and it was all that the two of us could do to lift him and load him into the back of it. We transported the deer back to the shack, and it took four of us to lift him up to secure him on the buck pole. My father arrived back for breakfast, admired my kill, and examined the carcass of the deer. He came to the conclusion that I had hit the deer a total of five times. In addition to the bullet to the deer's neck, one bullet had broken the deer's left front foreleg, a bullet had hit and broken the deer's spine just behind the front shoulders, and the other two bullets had landed solidly in the chest. There were no other wounds.

Later that evening, I was relating the tale of the hunt and going over every detail with all of the other hunters sitting around the table. Although I insisted that I had fired all eight bullets in my rifle and then reloaded and fired an additional five rounds, everyone was insisting that they had only heard five shots, not thirteen. The next morning, Peter walked back on Chicago Avenue and located the spot in the road where I had been standing when shooting at the deer. Although the snow had melted, it was easy for him to find the spot from which I had been shooting. He kicked around in the leaves and was able to find all thirteen of my shells. He brought them back to the shack with him when we all gathered for our late morning breakfast. He once again asked me, "How many times did you say you shot at that buck yesterday?" I responded, "Thirteen." He then gave me one of the biggest grins I've ever seen in my life and pulled the thirteen shells out of his pocket, laying them on the table. Five of the bullets were spent. The other eight bullets were still fully loaded. I sat there quietly and stared at the bullets. I had experienced "buck fever" and had been totally oblivious to that fact. I had indeed only fired five bullets. The other bullets had been ejected from my rifle without being fired. I obviously had been so excited that I was double- or triple- cocking my .30-30 as I was shooting at the deer.

We brought the deer into town at the end of deer season and stopped by the local feed mill to have it weighed. It dressed out at 232 pounds, and the width of the antlers was 24 inches. A true trophy. I cut the antlers off the head, mounted them on a wooden plaque, and returned them to the shack in the spring, where I nailed them above the entry door inside the shack for everyone to hang their hats on for good luck. That summer, a porcupine slid down the chimney connected to our wood cook stove. It entered the shack through the stove and chewed on everything it could sink his teeth into. Porkies love deer antlers, and my trophy rack is now only a memory.

Camp No-Hunt

Deer season 1964 was unusually cold, with sub-zero temperatures and very little snow cover. I shot a small buck at the Big Rock early opening afternoon, but no other deer were seen by the other hunters on that opening weekend.

It was becoming a tradition that on the first Sunday evening of the deer season, Camp No-Hunt would come to Blue Heaven to celebrate the hunt, or we would go over to their camp to be entertained.

Camp No-Hunt was also known as "Hunters, Inc." and, similar to the Jolly Boys, the members of their camp had taken advantage of the recreational use permits offered in the mid-1950s. They had built their own camp on Bayfield County Forest lands about ten miles west of our shack. The seven members of Camp No-Hunt were all prominent Hayward businessmen and were slightly older than the Jolly Boys. I don't know this to be true, but rumor had it that the members of their camp were forbidden to shoot any deer, and any member violating that rule would be banned from their hunting camp. I never remember any deer hanging from their buck pole, and there was never any sign that any deer had been hanging there.

Camp No-Hunt was a fun-loving, mischievous group of men; the biggest rascal was Orville "Dane" Nelson. In addition to his skills as a carpenter, Dane was also the first sergeant of the local National Guard unit, which was a combat engineer battalion. Dane had extensive knowledge and access to a multitude of devices with trip-wires, many with the capacity to generate loud explosive warnings that the enemy was approaching. One could never approach their camp unannounced, as Dane had affixed warning devices on the roadway to their camp, the areas surrounding it, and even the outhouse door. He was the self-appointed sergeant-at-arms for Camp No-hunt and took his position very seriously. He never showed up at our camp without wearing his first sergeant shirt and combat engineer beanie, and he never failed to make us roll with laughter.

One Sunday evening in 1964, the seven members of Camp No-Hunt arrived at Blue Heaven promptly at 5 p.m. They were all crammed into Harold Gobler's four-door Jeep Wagoneer, and they were ready to party. As usual, the road to our shack was in horrible condition. Although the temperature was well below zero, the large mud hole just below our shack had not completely frozen over because of the constant traffic it had seen on the opening weekend of deer season. Harold's Jeep was a muddy mess after crashing through the final mud hole to reach our shack.

The shack log from 11/22/64 recorded this:

"Big party at Bloo Heaven. Guests included the members of Camp No-Hunt, Fr. Bob Hanson, Bob Hanson, Vern Inhoff, Don Gillis and Curt Karbalis. Carl Bensen bled a little. Dane felt pretty bad. Wonderful party!"

As was the usual custom, there was a long happy hour, lots of snacks, and then a songfest until dinner was served. The menu included prime rib, crisp-skinned baked potatoes from the wood stove, shack peas, and salad. There were about 17 for dinner that evening, so the Jolly Boys had to serve dinner in shifts. When dinner was concluded, everyone said their goodbyes, and the members of Camp No-Hunt all piled into Harold's Jeep for the trip back to their shack. It was bitterly cold outside by that time. Harold put the vehicle in gear, but it wouldn't move; all four wheels on the vehicle were completely frozen from the water in the mud hole on the trip in.

Everyone pitched in to try to get the vehicle to move, but it wouldn't budge. Kenny even started up his Jeep to give Harold's vehicle a push, hoping that would free the wheels. Nothing worked. Finally, Harold became impatient, threw the vehicle in gear, and pressed the accelerator to the floor. Horrible odors came from that old Jeep as the transmission blew and the engine fried. The vehicle was toast. Ultimately, the Jolly Boys had to transport the Camp No-

Hunt members back to their shack. Harold's Jeep sat next to our shack for the rest of the deer season and was not returned to town until the road completely froze over so a wrecker could come in and pick it up. A lesson learned.

No further deer were seen during that week. It was too cold and nothing was moving. I returned to college that week but drove back to Hayward early on Friday for the final weekend. It was snowing heavily, and the temperatures had moderated. I stopped at Alexander & McGill's, where my father worked, advising him that I had arrived and would head up to the shack and walk in and get all the fires going. As I was leaving, he jokingly said, "Are you going out to hunt in this stuff?"

I responded, "I may just do that for an hour or two. There's plenty of new tracking snow, and I just may get on a hot track and shoot a deer and leave it on the steps for your arrival." I arrived at the shack about 3, started the oil burner, and got a roaring fire going in the wood cook stove. I was just going to sit there and enjoy the shack and its solitude but then decided to take a short walk back on Chicago Avenue to see if there was any activity or fresh tracks. I loaded my rifle and was on Chicago Avenue a short time later. I was examining the new snow on the ground to see if there were any fresh deer tracks and looked up. There before me in the heavily falling snow was a huge doe about 30 yards away. I pulled the rifle to my shoulder and killed her with one shot. I quickly field-dressed the deer and then realized that I had nothing with me to drag her back to the shack with me. I had never expected to see a deer and had left my dragging rope and most of my other gear back at the shack. I removed the belt from my pants, tied it around her neck, dragged her back to the shack, and laid her on the steps. About an hour later, it was dark and I could see the lights of the Coot coming towards the shack. I sat inside the shack and was giggling to myself, awaiting the reaction from the Jolly Boys when they came around the corner of the shack and discovered the deer on the steps. It was an unforgettable moment for me and one that my father talked about for many years afterward.

"Camp No-Hunt" (also known as "Fort Nelson") greet the "Jolly Boys" from "Blue Heaven" with song and drink on a Sunday evening during deer season. (L-R) Dane Nelson, Carl Nordquist, Bruce McGill (center), Carl Benson (standing), (unknown), Harold Gobler.

ANNUAL MEETING OF HUNTER"S INC. 1957

The first annual meeting of the Hunter's Inc. was held at the C.V. Benson residence on Dec. 27. 1957 at 8:00 P.M. with President Benson presiding. Members present were Carl Nordquist and Carl Benson. Members absent were: Harold Gobler, Orville Nelson, Harland Collett, Bruce McGill and Wilbur Shuman.

It was unanimously agreed that as C.V.Benson was the only successful male (Buck) with Horns Deer Slayer among the memebers of the Hunters Inc. he be President and the following slate of officers be sworn in office for the year 1957-58 and have full jurisdiction at the Lodge in Totogatic.

1. C.V.Benson--President
2. Harold Gobler--Past President, Secretary and Treasurer
Orville (Dane) Nelson--Past, Past President
4. Bruce (Nippy) McGill--Never, Never President
5. Harland (Heinie) Collett)--Bull Cook and custodian of the slot machin
6. Carl (Reddy) Nordquist--Has gun-will travel
7. Wilbur Shuman--Chief Jeep Driver--As hunter, time will tell.

The following change in By Laws was adopted:

1. Snoring must be limited to President Benson only.
2. Placing of bombs under toilet seat prohibited.
3. Gurgling of Intoxicating Liquors prohibited before breakfast on Saturday, Sunday, Monday, Tuesday, Wednesday, Thursday and Friday. Holi days and Goblers Birthday excepted. Liquor for gurgling purposes to be furnished by gurgler--(Heinie).
4. All Hunters (including McGill) to be out offcamp and ready for action by 11:30 A.M. on opening day of season
5. Card playing POSITIVELY prohibited during the hous of 4A.M. to 11 A.M. Adverse weather conditions may alter this decision of President Benson.
6. All members to remain seated and perfectly quiet during the following T.V. Programs:
   1. Gunsmoke, 2. Wyatt Earp, 3. Have Gun Will Travel
   4. Sheriff of Cochise, 5. Colt 45
7. Nordquist (Have Gun Will Travel) be permitted to have Jam and Preserv at his discretion.
McGill (nippy) to operate, Maintain and have full supply of gas, oil, and batteries for Kohler Plant (Light and Power) at all hours.
9. Dane (Carpenter Nelson) to have Deer (Buck) Rack ready on demand.
10. Past President Gobler (Gump) to bring back alive Water Buffalo seen by him somewhere in the Totogatic on or about Nov. 22, 1957.
11. Wilbur (Broken Ribs) Shuman to carry adequate liability insurance (Doctors and Hospitalization) while lying in bunk.

Full cooperation by all Members to the best of their ablity is expected at all times and under all ciecumstances.

APPROVED AND SEALED

C V Benson

C.V.Benson--President

(L-R) Adder Madson, Father Bob Hanson, Marv Hanson, Vern Inhoff and Kenny Sugrue dine on the dinner being served to them by members of "No-Hunt."

(L-R) Vern Inhoff, Marv Hanson, "Porky" Hanson, Merle Dunster and Adder Madson near the wood stove watching venison being fried.

Jolly Boys and Camp No-Hunt members and a few guests at Blue Heaven for a Sunday evening dinner. (From center, L-R) Marv Hanson, Adder Madson, Vern Inhoff, Merle Dunster, Carl Nordquist, Harold Gobler, Robert Dunster, Dane Nelson and Harry Erickson.

Deer Camps Remembered

Adder was the night owl of our hunting camp and was a great storyteller. He took pride in relating stories of the deer camps of yesteryear that could be found in our area during the years of the Great Depression and just prior to World War II. He had witnessed much of it and would sit at the table by the light of the Aladdin lamp late into the night, smoking his pipe, sipping on a snifter of brandy, and reciting his memories of being a part of those camps when he was a young man. He would describe in great detail the hardships the hunters endured back then. We'd listen intently to his tales of those days.

The deer camps of that era were very crude by today's standards. The hunters who occupied them all had the same mission: slay a deer and bring it home to help feed their families. They showed up with their well-oiled deer rifles and boots, wearing an assortment of worn, heavy wool clothing and had usually walked to the camp carrying the supplies they needed in a knapsack on their back. There were no shared meals back then. For the most part, everyone was there as an individual hunter and the only food shared would be fried venison heart or liver if someone was fortunate enough to shoot a deer. The hunters would bring their own personal supplies that they would need while they were at deer camp. It was simple fare, consisting of dried or canned meat, salt pork, beans, coffee, a few seasonings, lard for frying, and maybe a little moonshine or tobacco to enjoy before bedtime. The camps all had names, and most camps were named after a local landmark. Some of these camps did not have a specific owner. They had been built in the past by loggers or trappers for shelter and had been left abandoned for the use of anyone who wished to stay there.

The shelter in which they slept was made of logs with a dirt floor. The floor would become muddy as the heat from the stove thawed the ground inside the shack. They were constructed with the materials available from the surrounding woods. They were indeed what one would truly consider a "hunting shack." There were no frills, and the furnishings inside were sparse or non-existent. Ceilings were low, and the bunks had wood slates to hold straw used to cushion and insulate the bunk. No one had sleeping bags back then, using wool blankets instead. Heat was provided by a small pot-bellied stove which also served as a cooking surface that was shared by all. Frequently, the hunters would just eat from the cooking utensil rather than use a plate. There was no electricity or running water. The lighting was provided by oil burning lamps or candles, and water was obtained from a nearby creek or by melting snow. Even if facilities to do so had been available, it was too cold to bathe and there was no privacy in which to do so.

The hunters would be in the woods from the crack of dawn until it became too dark to see. Their evenings were spent mending their hunting gear, reading, or discussing the day's hunt or tales of trophy bucks taken in years past. Most would sit or lie around in their wool underwear while their hunting clothes dried out near the pot-bellied stove. During those times, it was a brotherhood formed out of necessity because of a common quest.

When I was in my early teens, I had the opportunity to experience one of those old hunting camps that my friends and I had discovered while partridge hunting north of Hayward in the Togatic Flowage area. It was located in the hardwoods about a half-mile off highway 27 about 12 miles north of town and had been built with large white pine logs into the side of a small hill. It had two small windows in the front, and the only door was still secure and hanging from leather straps that were used for hinges. We checked out the interior and found four double bunks, a hand-made table with several stools, and a pot-bellied stove which appeared to still still fully functional. It was dry inside, and it appeared that the tar-papered roof had not been leaking. Everything appeared to still be in reasonably good condition and habitable. We decided it would be fun to camp out there for a night, and several of my buddies and I talked my dad into giving us a ride up to the area the following weekend in his 1954 Chevrolet station wagon with our supplies. It was late fall, and the leaves had fallen off the trees. The days were mild, but at night the temperature fell into the low 30s. Our plan was to spend the day bird hunting in the area, stay overnight in the old shack, and have my father pick us up and return to town the next morning. We hiked into the old deer camp carrying our shotguns and sleeping bags, along with Kool-Aid, hot dogs and canned beans for our supper, and some candles for light at night. All of us thought that it was going to be a great adventure to spend a night in this old deer camp.

On arrival, we gathered enough firewood to start a fire in the stove and stockpiled enough wood to keep the place heated overnight. We cleaned up the place the best that we could. Although there were a few deer mice evident, we weren't concerned about their presence, as we knew there was little we could do to rid the place of them. I selected one of the upper bunks, unrolled my sleeping bag on the straw in the bunk, and jumped up in the bunk to "try it out." I closed my eyes momentarily and thought about what it must have been like to live in this old log cabin deep in the woods years ago. As I was lying there, I could hear some rustling close to me where the wall and roof joined together. I assumed I had probably invaded a space where some mice were nested but decided to have a closer look. There, lying about a foot away from me, was a four-foot-long bull snake. I shot out of that bunk like a launched missile and quickly pointed out my discovery to my companions. It was immediately agreed by all that given my discovery, it might not be wise for us to try to sleep overnight in those old bunks. We gathered our gear, hiked about two miles to a resort on Nelson Lake, and called my father, asking to be retrieved, as we were cancelling our planned outing.

Reflecting back on that episode, it was decided by all that that big bull snake ruled that old hunting shack and we were the intruders. He had found shelter and had plenty of deer mice to dine on, and we had no business attempting to invade his established territory.

Deer Camps of LK&Q

The Jolly Boys and Camp No-Hunt had formed a bond from the very beginning of the development of the two deer camps. No-Hunt was a colorful bunch of fun-loving guys which included Carl Benson, Harold Gobler, Bruce McGill, Heinie Collett, Carl Nordquist, Dane Nelson, and Wilbur Shuman. It was a social group, and there probably wasn't a serious deer hunter among them. It had become tradition that on the first Sunday night of the annual deer season, No-Hunt would either come to Blue Heaven to be entertained or we would go to their camp for an evening of festivities. There was always friendly competition between the camps to see who could do the best job of entertaining their visitors and who could serve up the best dinner at their camp.

Before moving forward any further, it is only fitting to give honorable mention to multiple other deer camps in our area. Many were on private lands, but a multitude of camps were also taking advantage of the recreational use permits being issued by Sawyer County. They too were a brotherhood of hunters, and the Jolly Boys and Camp No-Hunt did not have exclusive expertise in operating a successful hunting camp. Almost all had their own traditions and colorful names for identification and their own methods for building memories. Each deer season involved trying to communicate with many of the other deer camps as the deer season progressed to obtain reports on the success of the other hunters in the area. This accounting of some of the other deer camps in our area is only scratching the surface of the numerous deer camps that dotted the landscape. To provide a complete accounting is the subject matter for an entirely separate book.

To our immediate west were the hunters of "the Silver Dollar Club" and "Club 27." We didn't know the hunters from the Silver Dollar Club very well but knew they hailed from southern Wisconsin and hunted the county forest lands to their immediate west, so we seldom crossed paths in the woods. It was different with Club 27, since we would frequently see them in the woods during deer season, as they hunted just to the north of our camp. Frequently, Darrell Slama or Richard "Son of Beach" Schmitt would stop by at Blue Heaven to check out what was hanging on our buck pole and bring us up to date on who was hunting out of their camp that year and who had been successful in shooting a deer. To our south just off the Jolly Fisherman Road were several hunters from Minnesota. They called themselves "Minnesota Ridge," and we would run into them while hunting in the southern parts of our hunting area. To our east were all of my mother's relatives on Nelson Lake, hunting out of their cabin they called "Togi Bay." Adjacent to them was Norbert Reisterer and his sons Ron and Steve. They called their camp “Reisterer’s Roost.” The hunters from Togi Bay and Reisterer’s Roost hunted just on the fringes of the hunting area to our east, and it wasn’t unusual for any of these hunters to show up at our door to wet their whistle and check out what kind of success we were having during the deer hunt.

Farther to our north, situated along the Seeley Fire Lane and Duck Pond Road, were multiple deer camps. The Bushland and Gillis families both had camps on the Seeley Fire Lane. Bushland’s consisted of Lloyd Bushland and his son Forrest, along with other relatives and friends. The Gillis camp was called “Dynamite Hill” and was occupied by brothers Don and Dick Gillis along with their sons and Phil Barnes and Bob Mockler. To the west of these camps lay “Bare-naked Purgatory Swamp,” occupied by Ward, Ross, and Rolf Williamson and their friends Al Fuller and Rollin Swanson. There was also “Camp Handicapped,” so named because two of their members wore artificial limbs. Their camp members included my cousin, John “JK” Dunster; Rolf Williamson; Mike Kelsey; Al Fuller; Tom Graham; and Don Sahs.

One of the larger deer camps in our area was a concrete hunting cabin built by cement mason Ernie Anderson that they simply called “the Shack.” It was originally owned by Walt West, Bud Smith, Shorty Jensen, and Dick Wade. It ultimately became a family-oriented deer camp, complete with the luxury of a flush toilet. Over the years, it was occupied by Mike Sawyer, Ward Williamson along with his step-sons Jeremy and Eric Reek, Camp

Cook John Gregerson, Todd Williamson, Ross Williamson, "Snoball" Williamson, Wendy Williamson, Kyle Williamson, Pat Hand, Steve Sawyer, Bob Kramer, Rick Anderson, Rollin Swanson, Terry Johnson, Skip Brueggeman, Bob Woodbeck, Larry Mann, Tally Leslie, and many others. Ultimately, the owners became Ward Williamson, Mike Sawyer, Jeff Williamson and Greg Biskup. "The Shack" was well-known and popular in the area, and Game Warden Milt Dieckman would frequently visit the camp with his good friend Jay Reed, from the *Milwaukee Journal*, to take photos and write stories for his outdoor articles.

I also recall that the Brandt family had a large deer camp that had been in existence for years in the Lost Land Lake area, and there was also a camp known as "Red Ike," consisting of Haywardites Jack Moreland, Nate DeLong, Dick Swiler, George Rhenstrand, Basil Eastman, and Gordy Skamser. Word had it that Red Ike actually had a television set to watch the many football games being aired during deer season. It made one wonder how serious these guys were about "the hunt."

During the early years of Blue Heaven, Vern Inhoff had been a frequent guest of the Jolly Boys at various functions that were held up there. Vern was so impressed with the design and success of Blue Heaven that in 1970 he joined forces with his son Gary. They constructed their own hunting camp along with Bob and Rob Labarre, Arnie Anderson, Phil Barnes, Rick Anderson, Dave Henning and Don Primley Senior and Junior. They copied the design of Blue Heaven in the construction of their hunting camp, which was a great source of pride for the Jolly Boys.

Many of these deer camps are no longer in existence today, and the hunters that occupied them have moved on to hunt elsewhere after becoming victims of the termination of the recreational use permits which no longer allowed the camps on county forest lands.

The Boot Rack

They say that necessity is the mother of invention. Such was the case in the mid-1960s when Adder and I came up with a solution for all the wet boots scattered on the shack floor during the overnight hours.

Adder was known to all of us as the camp night owl. After the evening's activities had concluded, the light plant would be turned off and replaced by the soft glow of Aladdin lamps which had been lit and placed on the table. Many of the hunters would retire for the evening and head for their bunks, exhausted from the day's activities and looking forward to a good night's sleep and the next day's hunt. Not Adder. This was his favorite time of the day. He waited for this time of the evening and would pour a small shot of brandy to settle in at his favorite spot at the table and soak in the ambiance of the deer camp. Who could blame him? The Aladdin lamps gave off a soothing, dim yellow light. The only sound one could hear was the wood in the wood stove gently snapping, the tea kettles on the back of the stove barely hissing, and a few of the hunters gently snoring in their bunks. The shack was warm and cozy. It was a little slice of heaven at Blue Heaven.

Adder was the patriarch of the hunting camp, and everyone always took his council seriously. He was a force to be reckoned with at the poker table, and it was unusual when he didn't end up as one of the winners at the end of the evening. He had grown up in the Great Depression and had spent many deer seasons in the hunting camps of old that were now just memories. His stories of those days were fascinating, and he shared those with us into the late evenings. We learned how things were back then, and we were thankful to have so much more at our deer camp.

One such evening during the middle of deer season in the mid 1960's, Adder had taken his usual place at the table and invited me to stay up and have a nightcap with him. We had finished an excellent evening dinner of a garlic-laced pork roast complemented with squash and mashed potatoes prepared by my father, and Merle had made his famous oyster dressing and the gravy. Everyone else had already crawled into their bunks. I poured myself an after-dinner drink and sat down at the table with him. We shared stories of the events of that day and were enjoying the dim light of the Aladdin lamps when Adder decided that he should put more wood in the wood stove. As he walked by the oil burner next to the wood stove, he tripped over one of many boots that were lined up around the oil burner in a feeble attempt to dry them out before the next morning. He muttered a few swear words, finished the task of putting more wood on the fire, and returned to the table with a disgusted look on his face.

Adder said to me, "We have to do something about all the boots lying around on the floor in here. This place is too small for everyone leaving their boots lying around." I agreed and told him that I had been thinking about that issue for the last couple of years. I went on to say that what we needed was a boot rack hung in the rafters high above the oil burner and wood stove to store and dry all of the boots. It is common knowledge that heat rises and cold air falls. Even though our shack is not insulated, the wood stove provides great warmth, with the inside shack temperature at 80 degrees. At night, the small oil burner keeps the interior temperature from freezing, but in the morning, the interior temperature is 45 or 50 degrees. The hunting boots would still be wet and were always cold by morning.

The hunting boots back then were what people called "packs." They had rubber bottoms with upper leather tops that laced. A hunter could purchase felt insoles for them, but after he spent a day stomping around in the woods, the inside of the boots would always be wet from sweating feet or stepping in water. At night, the hunters piled them by the oil burner in an effort to dry them out. It was futile, and the inside of the boots was still wet and also cold from sitting on the uninsulated floor overnight.

That night on a piece of scratch paper, Adder and I designed and invented the camp boot rack. Adder was an excellent carpenter and had a woodworking shop in his basement at home. It was a simple design. Large spikes would be hammered into pre-drilled holes about three inches apart in an eight-foot two-by- four. The nail heads of the spikes would then be sawed off with a hacksaw, and then the two-by-four would be nailed or wired up in the rafters above the stoves. Boots could then be inserted and hung upside-down between the spikes.

Adder returned to camp the Friday after Thanksgiving with the newly constructed boot racks. He had made three of them. Each rack could hold up to eight pairs of boots. We installed the boot racks that afternoon, and each hunter slid his wet boots into the rack at the end of that day's hunt along with his wet gloves and wool socks. The next morning, everyone had dry, warm boots. The invention and success of the boot rack is still a topic of conversation today when we hang up our boots for the night.

The following deer season Adder brought in eight individual wood storage lockers that he had constructed to be used by the hunters to store their surplus gear which previously had been stowed in the bunk area. He had secretly obtained the necessary measurements during the previous deer season, and six of the lockers were stacked into one unit, with the other two stacked in another. There was much debate over who would use which locker, and the Jolly Boys went into "Executive Session" to make that decision. This innovation was welcomed by all and allowed each hunter to have easy access to all of his spare equipment and small personal belongings. On occasion, the Jolly Boys would hold locker inspections to ensure that everyone's locker was orderly and contained the essential contents for a successful deer hunt. There is more than one kind of "boot camp."

"The Boot Rack" with about 16 pairs of boots hanging upside down above the wood cook stove and oil burner while drying out and warming wet boots. We consider this innovation our best invention at our hunting camp.

Adder's individual storage lockers set in place at the entrance to the bunk area. Hunters use this space to stow their smaller items and keep things organized.

The Nightly Card Games
Poker and Cribbage

During the long, dark evening hours of deer season, many hunting camps pass the time with card games of poker or cribbage. Our camp is no exception. The game of choice would normally be poker, but on occasion there would only be two or three hunters in camp at night, so the game of the evening would be cribbage, which only requires two to four players.

From the beginning, the Jolly Boys decided that any card games played at the shack needed to have limitations and rules to keep things from getting out of control. The last thing anyone wanted to see was someone losing or winning a lot of money at the card table and bad feelings developing between the hunters. The evening card games were to provide entertainment and camaraderie until it was time to serve the evening meal. The Jolly Boys wanted the card games to be friendly, and there were "shack rules" concerning the stakes and rules of play. If a "shack rule" did not specifically address the situation, the Book of Hoyle would be consulted.

The first rule addressed stakes. They would play "nickel-dime" poker, meaning that each poker chip would equal five cents, and the poker chips would be purchased from an individual designated as the "banker" for the evening. The ante and maximum bet on seven-card games would be limited to five cents. On five-card games, the stakes were limited to ten cents for the ante and bets. A maximum of only three raises would be allowed in each betting session. Keeping the stakes at nickel-dime would restrict winnings or losses to around ten dollars per evening for a player, no matter how lucky or unlucky they might be on any particular evening. The Jolly Boys recognized that everyone at the poker table had different incomes, and they wanted to include and encourage the younger hunters to also play in the poker games. To assist the inexperienced players, a rule was established that "the cards speak for themselves." At the end of each game, the players who had remained in the game would turn their cards over and declare their hands. On occasion, an inexperienced player would declare his hand and one of the more experienced players would recognize that the hand being shown was actually higher than what the player had declared. Had this rule not been applied, there would have been many a winning hand thrown in by the inexperienced player and the pot lost by the actual winner. If no one called a bet and there was only one player remaining in the game, it wasn't necessary for that player to show everyone else what he had in his hand.

The poker games would be "dealer's choice." Everyone had a favorite game that they thought they had the best chance at winning, so a wide variety of different games could be played on any given evening. The evening poker game would start as soon as all of the hunters had come in from the woods, changed clothes, and put out snacks for everyone's enjoyment. Everyone playing would normally purchase about two dollars' worth of chips from the banker, and whoever had been the big winner the previous evening had the duty to deal out cards face-up to everyone playing until a jack appeared. Whoever received the first jack had the privilege of dealing the first card game and also had to verify that all chips purchased had been paid for if there wasn't a designated banker for the evening.

There have been many different poker games introduced and played at the poker table at our camp, but many of those games were only played once or twice because they were too complex and didn't become popular with those at the poker table. Frequently, the dealer would have to modify the game slightly if there were numerous players at the table and not enough cards to play his favorite game. This was easily accomplished by limiting the number of cards a player could draw in five-card games or by reducing the number of cards dealt to a player in the stud games. When there are seven players sitting at the table, it's very difficult to deal five-card draw without limiting the draw to two cards per player. When there are more than seven players, most draw games and seven-card stud games are impossible to play, as there are not enough cards in the deck.

There isn't enough space in this book to describe all of the various card games that we've played at the poker table at our hunting camp over the years, and most of these games and their descriptions can be found in any good book on poker. The most frequently played games at our poker table are five-card draw with deuces wild, and a game called "baseball." This is a seven-card stud game with threes and nines wild, one has to pay extra for a wild three if it is dealt face up. A player getting dealt a four up also gets a free card dealt to him face down. Baseball is one of our favorite games, and the winner of the game usually wins a rather significant pot when the game is concluded. We also play five-card draw with fives and tens wild, which is a game called "dime store." Playing poker games with so many wild cards usually requires a rather high hand to win the game, and it's not unusual to have several players holding four-of-a-kind or a straight flush.

On occasion, we will play a five-card game called "spit in the ocean." The dealer will designate one of the players to say "spit" while four cards are being dealt face down to the players. When the word "spit" is shouted by the designated person, the dealer turns up a card from the deck and places it at the center of the table. That card (and all others like it) is wild. The card that was "spit" serves as the fifth card in everyone's hand. A player can draw two cards, and the best five cards in this game wins. We also like a game called "3-3-3." Three cards are dealt face-up, and three cards are dealt face-down, with threes being wild.

My favorite poker game is a seven-card stud game called, "low hole card is wild and all others like it." I find it to be challenging, because two cards are dealt face-down, four are dealt face-up, and the seventh and final card is dealt face-down. That final card being dealt face-down can change the complexion of your hand. It can either make or break your chances of winning, especially if you started the game with a pair of fours dealt to you face-down on the onset of the game and then a lower card is dealt to you on the final face-down card. Most people playing this game stick it out to the end, and it usually takes a relatively high hand to win the game. The best five cards of the seven are used when declaring the poker hand. The dealer always carefully monitors this game to make certain that the face-down cards are being carefully separated from the face-up cards and are not commingled.

In the mid-1960s, my father's youngest brother, Bobby Hanson, began to hunt with us, as his hunting group had disbanded and we had a spare bunk for him to occupy. Bobby lived in Superior, Wisconsin, and always referred to himself as "The Superior Card Player." He loved to play poker and cribbage. Bobby was a Certified Public Accountant and had a gift for playing cards and playing cards well. If you were playing cribbage with him, more often than not he had your hand counted before you even laid down your cards to count them yourself. He would say, "Take your 12" or "Take your 14" while you were still trying to determine how many cribbage points you had in your hand.

When Bobby arrived at camp, he introduced a new poker game to the Jolly Boys and the other hunters that he called "red dog." In most poker circles, this poker game is called "guts." It quickly became our favorite game because of its simplicity and the fact that it's a game where one can "bluff" and end up winning the pot, as well as the fact that it can be played by a large group.

Red dog is dealt by the dealer after calling for an ante to be put in the center of the table by each player. The ante can be a nickel, dime, or even a quarter, with each player playing to try to win the money in the pot. The players all agree on how large the initial ante should be. Two cards are dealt to each player face-down. The big advantage to this game is that there are no limitations concerning how many players are at the table, as the deck has 52 cards and each player only receives two cards, so there could be up to 26 players playing this game. It's a great poker game to play when there is a large group gathered around the poker table. The other advantage is that one does not require a great deal of poker knowledge or skill to play the game, as the game is simply won by the player having the two best cards. Suits and runs don't count in this game, a pair of aces is the highest hand, and any pair is a great hand. Once all the players have their two cards, it's time for each player to declare if he is staying in to play for "the pot" or folding his hand and waiting for a more opportune time for his chance to win. The declaration to play is announced by each player by saying either "in" or "out," and the first player to the left of the dealer is the first to declare. That is referred to as "being under the gun." Then, every other player has the opportunity to declare in or out, which is done in a clock-wise fashion around the table. If only one player has declared that he is in, he wins the money in the pot, the game is over, and the deal passes to the next dealer. If everyone at the table has declared to be out, the dealer cannot say "in" and win the pot unless the dealer has an ace or higher in his hand. If no one has stayed and the dealer doesn't have an ace or better, the dealer reshuffles the cards and re-deals, and the game starts anew. Usually, there will be two or more players that declare to be in and there can be only one winner. If two have declared to be in, the player with the higher poker hand wins, and the loser matches the pot. Often a player might stay in with just a king and another card, attempting to bluff and win the pot. As everyone declares whether they are in or out, the players sitting the closest to the dealer after most of the players have made their intentions known to others as to whether they are in or out have the best opportunity to bluff with their hands. Frequently, everyone will declare that they are "out," and the only two remaining to declare in or out are the dealer and the person sitting to the dealer's immediate right. The player sitting on the dealers right often will try to "buy" the pot by bluffing and will say that he's in even though he may only be holding two very low cards. If the dealer also has a low hand, the dealer will usually fold rather than taking the chance to "keep the other player honest" and calling the bluff. The players or players that have lost have to match the amount of money that's in the pot, and there's a real kicker to this game: there are no ties. If two players have exactly the same hands, like an ace-ten, they both lose even though they might have the highest hands and have to match the pot. If only two players are in and staying during each round, the pot will stay the same, as there is only one loser that matches the pot. However, if more than two players are in, the pot will double or even triple in size very quickly because if three players have stayed in, the winner gets only the amount in the pot, and the two losers then have to put in the amount of the pot, which would double the pot for the next game. The Jolly Boys, in keeping with their philosophy of keeping the poker stakes reasonable, quickly recognized this and established a two-dollar win-or-lose limit for the players. As a result, the most anyone can pull from the pot after a win is two dollars, and the most anyone has to put in if they lose is two dollars. Even with that shack rule, the money in the pot can quickly become a substantial amount, and the only way the pot can be "cleared" is if only one person stays and the amount in the pot is less than two dollars. Often one game of red dog can last for a very lengthy time if several players are constantly staying in.

Everyone always looks forward to the nightly poker games, as they not only provide a great source of entertainment but are also a good time to share stories of the day's hunt, plan the next day's hunt, talk politics, or discuss a variety of other topics while the cards are being shuffled between the games. I have stated that, in my opinion, shack life was 80% of deer hunting. I am also of the opinion that the nightly card games are 80% of shack life.

The poker game will usually last from about five in the afternoon until eight or nine in the evening. When everyone mutually decides on the appropriate time to terminate the poker game, one of the players will be designated to be the last dealer before everyone cashes in their chips. That person is given the honor of dealing one final game called "showdown."

"Showdown" is a great way to end an evening of poker. It provides an opportunity for someone that has lost at cards that evening to recover some of his losses or for one of the winners to increase his winnings. By agreement among all of the players at the table, an ante of twenty-five or fifty cents (and sometimes even up to a dollar) is placed in the center of the table. The designated dealer will then deal each player five cards one at a time and all face-up for everyone to see. When the deal is completed, the player with the highest poker hand showing wins the showdown proceeds.

Following dinner and cleaning up the kitchen area, the majority of the hunters would head for their bunks, but there were always a few die-hards who wanted to stay up for a bit longer for a "night cap" and engage in a game or two of cribbage by the light of the Aladdin lamps. Most up there were good at playing the game, which accommodates two, three, or four players. Cribbage is also played late in the afternoon before everyone is ready to sit down for the nightly poker game. The Jolly Boys also designated shack rules for the stakes of the cribbage games. They established that the winner would be entitled to receive twenty-five cents and fifty cents for "skunk." They maintained a rule that if a player had a blank hand, the player would have to pay a ten-cent penalty to every other player. The blank-hand payment has been abolished from the rules, as everyone eventually agreed that it wasn't right to penalize someone for not having any points in his cribbage hand.

One stormy day back in the mid 1970s there were six of us in camp. We had all returned to camp by mid-afternoon because we had a mixture of heavy, wet snow and freezing rain, and the conditions made it almost impossible to hunt. We decided that it would be a great afternoon to stay in the shack and just relax. Dennis Clagett opted to crawl into his upper bunk with a candle and a book he had brought along to read and also to listen to the rain on the roof. I was occupying myself by taking care of a few kitchen chores, and the other four guys decided to play a little cribbage while sipping on some tap beer until it was time for the poker game to get underway. The cribbage game that ensued was the usual competitive game, with Russ and Bobby as partners taking on my father and Adder as partners. There was much vocalizing in the game, and I noticed that Dennis had come out of his bunk and grabbed a pen and writing pad from the shelf to take back to his bunk. I didn't know what he was up to until later that afternoon, when he showed me his scribbled notes on the pad. Dennis, who had never played a hand of cribbage in his life, had become fascinated with various phrases and comments being made by the four cribbage players as they sat there playing their game and had written down what he was hearing for future reference. I share his comments, slightly edited, with all my fellow cribbage lovers, who will know instantly what each phrase or comment means:

1. Look at the cut that ***hole got!
2. No f****** ice! (meaning that the ice bucket was empty....again....)
3. What am I supposed to do with this s***!
4. Sonofabitch... What am I supposed to do with this f****** mess?
5. I have 20. F*** ya....
6. You p****!!
7. Knock...Knock...Knock...Knock (sound of players hitting their knuckles on the table instead of saying "go".)
8. Oh, s***!!
9. Whose play?!
10. Too f*****' many....
11. Whose crib?
12. I need a cut....
13. C*********! F***** either way. (Referring to discarding for the crib.)
14. What kind of s*** is this?!
15. This is f****** unbelievable!
16. Who dealt this s***?
17. This sucks...
18. What in the f*** are you doing with that card?

Sound familiar?

Russell "Dennis" Clagett lying in his upper bunk in mid-afternoon reading a book by candle light, sipping on a drink, and listening to the others sitting at the table playing cribbage while a storm releases its fury during deer season.

The three Hanson brothers (L-R) Kenneth, Bobby, and Jolly Boy Marvin playing a late night game of three-handed cribbage while enjoying an after-dinner cigar and some tap beer from the hand-crafted beer dispenser shown in the background which was made by Adder's brother Carl. The beer tapper was nicknamed "Carl."

A poker game in the late 1950s. (L-R) Adder Madson, (unknown), Howard Nystrom, Adrian Faase, Merle Dunster (standing), (unknown), Harry Erickson and Porky Hanson.

Mid-1960s poker game with participants (L-R) Dennis Clagett, Russ Clagett, Adder Madson, Marvin Hanson (stacking his winnings), Merle Dunster and Bobby Hanson who is preparing to deal the next hand.

The Dog Robber

No respectable hunting shack should be without a functional slot machine to entertain the hunters and raise revenue for camp operations. As good fortune would have it, Adder was able to find an old twenty-five-cent slot machine buried in the basement of the old Peoples National Bank. He brought it home and spent countless hours renovating it to make it functional. Fearful that someone would break into the shack and steal this antique, Adder would lug the machine to the Blue Heaven each deer season and lug it back home again for storage when the season had concluded. The Jolly Boys aptly nicknamed it "the dog-robber" after the old military term for a general's "lackey" who was utilized to fix problems or make them go away.

The Jolly Boys and all their guests at Blue Heaven would pump quarters into it, hoping to hit a jackpot to pay for their hunting trip, but Adder had the slot machine screwed down so tightly that it seldom spit out more than a quarter or two as winnings. The exception to that was in the mid-1960s, when my dad's brother Bobby and his friend George paid a visit to the camp just as we were about to sit down for our breakfast brunch. Being good hosts, we welcomed them, made them a Bloody Mary, and invited them to join us for brunch. George walked over to the slot machine and started putting quarters into it and pulling the lever. On his third quarter, the slot machine that never paid spilled its guts, and quarters came flowing out of it. All of us were in disbelief. He had hit the mother lode and had the unmitigated gall to ask for a coffee can to haul away his winnings. All of the Jolly Boys were in shock that George didn't return a portion of his winnings to them. George was talked about for some time to come about having walked away with revenue that had been meant for the shack operations fund. It goes without saying that my father's brother was chastised for bringing George into our camp, and George was banned for life from ever again setting foot in our hunting camp.

Jolly Boy Merle Dunster in his "tidy-white-eez" putting some of his poker winnings into the "Dog Robber" before retiring for the evening.

Lost in the Woods–1965

In the fall of 1964, Merle showed up driving a new toy that had been given to him by a close friend of his called a "Tri-Scat." It was a three-wheeled motorized tricycle powered by a 5-horsepower engine, with two large rear tires and a smaller front tire. It sat very low to the ground and was one of the forerunners of the all-terrain

Marvin Hanson admires Dennis Clagett's buck shot on Thanksgiving morning while Barbara Clagett readies her camera to photograph the event. The "Tri-Scat" was used by Dennis to drag the deer back to Blue Heaven. We frequently celebrated Thanksgiving at the shack with family members invited for the day.

vehicles which would be flooding the recreational market in the years to come. We were able to put the Tri-Scat into service immediately, hauling supplies into the camp and dragging deer back to the shack during deer season. It could transport only one person and wasn't that great in the snow, but it served its purpose and could avoid all the mud holes in the road leading into the shack.

The Tri-Scat was pressed into service on a rescue mission that year to locate one of our hunters who had gotten lost. My father and Merle had grown up with Sammy Helms in Hayward. The three of them had all enlisted in the Navy during World War II, and Sammy had become an aviator. After the war was over, Sammy elected to make the Navy his career and became close friends with another aviator, Robin "Bob" Larson. For a number of years, Sammy and Bob would fly into Hayward for the fishing season opener in a Navy Beechcraft Super 18, which was a very loud two-engine airplane. They would always "buzz" Hayward on their arrival, and my dad and Merle would rush out to the airport to pick them up. During deer season 1965, Sammy couldn't make it to Wisconsin for deer-hunting season, so Bob was invited to come up by himself. Bob was an avid hunter, known for taking frequent trips out West to hunt mule deer, elk, and other large game. He also was an avid fisherman and owned a small cabin in Canada, spending much of his free time in the summer up there fishing. He certainly wasn't a stranger to the woods, and we all regarded him as a part of our group and felt he would be a welcome addition at the shack.

Bob arrived early Friday afternoon to help haul in supplies and get the shack opened up for deer season. About 3:30 that afternoon, he decided to take a "short walk" to see if he could locate Merle's deer stand called the Birch, which was just south of the main logging road, in order to scout the area for deer sign in the snow that had fallen a few days before our arrival. By 4:30 it was dark and he wasn't back. Several of us went outside and shouted his name, hoping he would hear us, but we didn't get a response. We were all getting very concerned, as he should have been back before dark and we knew that he had left lightly dressed, with no rifle, flashlight, or compass. About 5 p.m., we fired a couple of shots into the air, hoping he would hear the gunshots, get his bearings, and find his way back. We then took the jeep and drove down to the area of the Birch. We did find his tracks in the snow where he had entered the woods, but there was no sign of him and no response when we yelled his name. Knowing that Merle was arriving shortly with the Tri-Scat, we went back to the shack to organize a search party. When Merle and my dad showed up about 6:30 that evening, we informed them that Bob was apparently lost in the woods without a flashlight or compass. Merle dressed in his warm hunting clothes and left camp about 7 p.m. with Adder's son Phillip to locate his tracks and follow them by Tri-Scat. They returned about 8:30 that evening with Bob in tow. He was cold, hungry, and very thirsty, but no worse for wear. We learned that when Bob got turned around in the woods and realized he was lost, he decided to do the smart thing and stay where he was, build a fire, and wait for us to find him. Although he had heard us firing our rifles, he had no way to respond to us and was fearful of falling and injuring himself if he attempted to walk through the woods in the dark. That evening, Bob made "mooseballs" from hamburger that he had brought with him from a moose he had shot in Canada that fall. We all enjoyed a very late dinner that evening and gave thanks that things had turned out well. There was much discussion that evening about what to do when lost in the woods. We managed to fill a couple of party tags that season but were unsuccessful in getting any bucks. Still, we declared the season a success, as everyone had returned from camp safely.

Deer Seasons 1966-1967

By the deer season of '66, the Jolly Boys had developed to perfection their signature style of hunting and entertaining themselves while at deer camp. Once again, the Jolly Boys hosted a huge party on the first Sunday evening of the hunt. There were 20 people cramped in that little cabin for an evening of cocktails, deer stories, and a lot of singing. A standing prime rib roast was served for dinner, complemented with baked potatoes, shack peas, salad, and a side dish made with sautéed mushrooms, green peppers, and onions. It had become tradition that Camp No-Hunt would visit our camp to be entertained for the evening, or we would motor over to their camp to be entertained. I was a youngster by their standards, and my role was more of an observer than a participant in all of the frolicking, but it was very obvious that the Jolly Boys and Camp No-Hunt had a friendly competition concerning which camp could be more entertaining. That year had been a buck only-party permit season, and although deer weren't plentiful in our area, we had still managed to down two bucks and a party doe for camp meat.

The following year was one that my father would never forget. At that time, I was employed as a young rookie cop working as a patrolman for the Eau Claire Police Department at night so I could take college courses during the day. I had been unable to get off work for deer season until midnight of the evening prior to the big day. Thanks to all the adrenaline running through me in anticipation of the big hunt, I had no problem staying awake for the two-hour drive from Eau Claire up to the hunting shack in the wee morning hours. I stumbled my way into the shack in pitch darkness carrying all my hunting gear. Everyone else was sound asleep on my arrival, but my father greeted me as I was crawling into my bunk about 3 a.m. I was hoping for at least a couple of hours of sleep before the alarm clock sounded. At 5 a.m., everyone awoke to the horrible blaring of Merle attempting to play reveille on a bugle that he had smuggled in. He had no problem drowning out the alarm clock which had also begun to ring to summon us to the hunt.

It was going to be a great day to be in the woods hunting. The temperature was relatively mild, with very little wind, and there was a snow cover of about four inches. My father announced that he was going to go up past the "Little Rocks" and position himself on a stump overlooking a large green swamp just west of the "Big Rock." I told him that I would hunt just north of him and attempt to push some deer in his direction. About mid-morning, I heard three shots coming from the area where he had posted himself and headed in that direction. I found him sitting on a stump, with a big cigar in the corner of his mouth. When I reached him, I whispered, "Did you get him?" He took the cigar from his mouth and whispered back, "Nope. Nice buck. Running full speed. Shot three times and can't figure out how I missed him."

We both headed back to shack to join the others for our noon brunch. That afternoon, my father decided to go back and reposition himself on his stump and sit there until it got dark. About 4 p.m., I heard another three shots coming from the area where he was, but there was no whistling or any other signals indicating he needed help, so I didn't walk over to the area where he was. When we met up a short while later back at deer camp, I asked him, "Was that you shooting again?" He responded, "Had a standing buck that had walked up within 75 yards of me. Shot at him three times and he finally turned and ran away." I could tell he was dismayed, as he was an excellent shot and seldom missed. Even though I already knew the answer, I asked him if had sighted in his deer rifle prior to deer season. He replied, "Too busy for that."

I put up a target, took his .30-30, and fired three shots. All three bullets struck the target high and to the right about two feet off center at 50 yards. He had somehow bumped his rear sight and had shot over the top of the two deer that he had seen that day. A lesson learned. Always test-fire your deer rifle before opening day.

The "Coot"

The most difficult part of getting the camp ready for deer season would be hauling in the supplies from the highway to the hunting shack on the three-quarter-mile logging road. The road was almost always wet, with deep mud holes and in a near-impassable condition. Would we get stuck? Would one of the old jeeps we used have mechanical problems? Would the road be clear of fallen trees? On numerous occasions, our arrival at camp would be delayed for any of these reasons, but the Jolly Boys always showed optimism and would quip, "It keeps other hunters and the game wardens from wandering back in here." Transportation in and out of the camp was always a problem, and the shack log reflects that in numerous entries. All of this would change with the arrival of the "Coot."

Merle had become acquainted with a summer Cable resident named Adrian Faase, who was from Omaha, Nebraska. Adrian and his wife, Flowell, had a summer home on Cable Lake. Merle and Gloria became very close friends with Adrian and Flowell, and Merle enjoyed showing off Blue Heaven to them. Adrian and Flowell were guests for a dinner party at the shack in the fall of

1959, and they experienced first-hand the transportation difficulties on the muddy logging road.

Adrian owned a company in Omaha called SnowCo, which manufactured a variety of farm equipment and trailers. In the mid-1960s, Adrian was contacted by a company that had designed a new four-wheel all-terrain vehicle that they were calling the "Coot." They needed a trailer to transport this newly designed vehicle and SnowCo was awarded the contract. In order to design the trailer, the manufacturer provided SnowCo with one of their machines. The trailer was designed, built, and put into production. The Coot manufacturer informed Adrian that he could keep the Coot, and the first thought in Adrian's mind was that this would be the perfect mode of transportation to traverse the muddy road into the hunting shack. In the summer of 1968, Adrian transported the Coot and its trailer to Cable and gave it to Merle as a gift.

The Coot was about the size of a small WWII jeep without a cab or a hood. It was a full-time 4-wheel-drive vehicle with two separate body sections that articulate, allowing all four wheels to be in contact with the ground at all times. It wasn't powered by a regular vehicle engine. It came equipped with an 18-horsepower Tecumseh engine, and the drive system was powered through a centrifugal clutch, very similar to a snowmobile. The Coot was geared for power and could easily push over a four-inch aspen tree and drive it through heavy brush. They were built to last, with a laminated all-steel frame welded to a 16-gauge steel skin. They were heavy and almost indestructible, and it was like driving a small tank through the woods. They were also designed to be amphibious, much like the WWII "Ducks." We once took it for a test drive on a lake. Although the tires only generated a speed of a couple of miles per hour, it did indeed float but was difficult to steer and maneuver. The Coot was designed with a centrifugal clutch, with a low gear and high gear for forward movement and one reverse speed.

Although this was the perfect piece of equipment to navigate the muddy logging road in and out of our hunting camp, it did have a few design drawbacks. It wasn't equipped with brakes; one simply took his foot off the accelerator and allowed it to roll to a stop. Normally, this was never a problem, but I recall one incident when we were hauling firewood and going up a hill in high gear. The Coot was losing power and coming to a stop, and during our attempt to move the transmission to low gear, the Coot began to roll rapidly backward. It was a harrowing ride until we came to a stop at the bottom of the hill, and we were thankful that the incident hadn't resulted in any injuries. From that day on, we made certain that we had the Coot in low gear before ascending or descending a hill with a full load. Another issue was turning radius. Although the Coot had a steering wheel and steered like a car, the turning radius was very limited, as the front wheels would rub up against the body of the vehicle when the driver attempted to turn in small circles. It therefore wass necessary to plan turns well in advance, similar to an 18-wheeler turning a sharp corner. There was no suspension on a Coot. When Merle was operating the Coot, he did so at one speed: wide open! Whenever we ran over a log or rock, everyone would bounce up off their seats and come crashing down with a jolt. Frequently, the ride would be painful, and everyone pleaded for a slow ride when Merle was behind the wheel.

Our Coot is still in service today. It has been mechanically rebuilt several times over the course of its service to our hunting camp and continues to be completely functional. It would be very difficult to estimate the tons of cargo that this machine has hauled in and out of the hunting shack over the course of the last forty years. The front section of the Coot has a bench seat and provides room for only the driver and one passenger. However, the rear portion is designed to carry cargo or up to four passengers. We have also added a small trailer that can be pulled to haul additional cargo.

Since 1968, this Coot has been our primary source of transportation and has hauled countless hunters and their gear, deer, and camp supplies. It has been an all-weather-and-terrain vehicle, and we've equipped the four wheels with chains for added traction. The only time the Coot has been stuck is when the driver has high-centered the Coot on frozen dirt above the ruts in the road. Today, we also use 4-wheel-drive 4-wheelers in addition to the Coot, since 4-wheel-drive pick-ups and SUVs still get stuck trying to traverse the mud holes to the shack.

In the mid-1980s, they stopped manufacturing the Coot, but of those that were built, many are still in operation today.

The "Coot" gets its maiden voyage into Blue Heaven in the fall of 1968. Merle is behind the wheel and Adder is riding "shotgun" with Marv in the back. Violet Hanson is standing in the door looking on.

Riding out after a day spent at the shack. (L-R) "Puffin" Sugrue, Merle, Ellen Madson, Kenny Sugrue and Adder with his shotgun.

THE BUNNY GIRLS ENTERTAIN

There were no shack log entries made for deer season 1968 by any of the Jolly Boys, which nonetheless turned out to be one to remember. The shade that we pull down which records all the deer kills indicates that we were successful in harvesting five deer that season. I shot a six-point buck at the Big Rock and also shot a couple of large does. A couple of the other hunters were also successful in bagging a deer.

My father called me a few weeks prior to the season opener, asking me to learn how to play "Bye-Bye, Blackbird" on my trumpet and to bring it up to the hunting shack on opening weekend. I had played the trumpet in high school and was actually quite proficient at it back then, but it was now buried in a closet somewhere and I hadn't touched it for years. I asked my dad what was going on. All he would tell me was that the Jolly Boys were planning on some special entertainment when the hunters from "Camp No-Hunt" arrived on Sunday night for the annual party between the two deer camps. It was a secret and he wouldn't say any more. It took some effort, but I learned to play the song and brought my trumpet up to deer camp.

After the opening day of hunting was over, my dad asked that I play the "Bye-bye, Blackbird" song for him and the other Jolly Boys. I pulled out my trumpet and played the song. It met with their approval, and they thanked me for learning to do it. But the rest of us hunters were still in the dark as to what the Jolly Boys were up to. Sunday arrived, and after hunting until about three that afternoon, we were all asked to come back to camp early to prepare for the big party with Camp No-Hunt. The shack was cleaned up, personal gear was stowed away, snacks were put out on the counter, and a huge prime rib roast was prepped to be put into the oven with scrubbed baked potatoes. In addition to the members of Camp No-Hunt, a multitude of others had been invited to this party, so we knew that the shack would be wall-to-wall with people and everyone would have to take turns at the dinner table. There were at least twenty of us in attendance for the party that evening.

Everyone arrived. Cocktails were served, snacks were consumed, and deer stories were told. It was definitely a party atmosphere. My dad and the other three Jolly Boys suddenly disappeared into the bunk area and pulled the curtains behind them. We all wondered what they were up to and heard lots of laughter and commotion going on behind the curtains. A few minutes later my dad stuck his head out from behind one of the curtains and motioned for me to join them. When I entered the bunk area, their "secret" became known to me. The four of them were all dressed as Playboy Bunny girls. My mother had designed the bunny girl costumes for them using old bras and stuffing them. She had sewn a large bunny tail on the back side of the underwear of each of the Jolly Boys and had also made each a headband with rabbit ears. The costumes were dyed blue in honor of Blue Heaven and the four of them stood there, their unshaven chests and legs for all the world to see. It was showtime.

My father told me to grab my trumpet from my bunk area and go out and play "Bye-bye, Blackbird." I did so, and the four of them parted the curtains and came out of the bunk area kicking up their legs in unison and singing a song they had written for the event to the melody of the song I was playing:

"Soooooooooo.......
Back your ass against the wall, here we come, balls and all...
Welcome No-Hunt....
Wiggle your tits and shake your ass, grab yourself an empty glass, Welcome No-Hunt....
We bunny girls are here to please you, with our costumes we will tease you...
Sooooooooooo.......
Back your ass against the wall, here we come, balls and all....Welcome No-Hunt."

The entertainment was a huge success, and they were asked to do two encores. It was an event that was to be talked about for years to come, and to this day no other entertainment or costume or merriment has matched those antics.

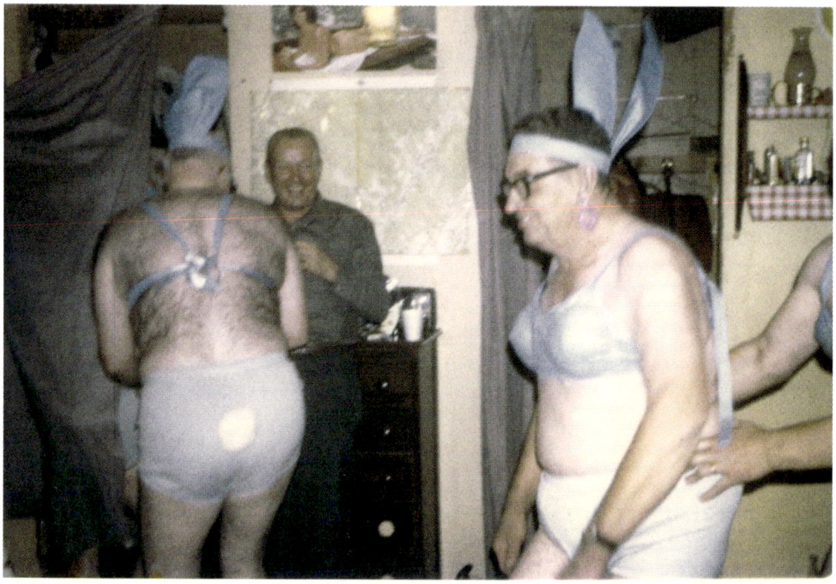

The Jolly Boys bunny girl show begins with their opening tune and dance while Bob Larsen tries to stay out of their way during the spectacle.

Jolly Boys (L-R) Marvin, Adder, Merle and Kenny present one of their many show tunes during their bunny girl show for Camp No-Hunt and other guests.

Reali Spaghetti

I love spaghetti with a great spaghetti sauce. Served with toasted garlic bread, an Italian salad, and a fine red wine, it's one of my favorite meals.

My sister, Marilynn, married DeLarry "Larry" Joseph Reali (pronounced "Ree-al-ee") in 1959. Larry was the son of Carl and Lesla Reali, and the family was of Italian-French heritage. They possessed an Old World recipe for spaghetti sauce that had been kept a family secret for years. It had been passed down from generation to generation, and whenever Larry visited us, we all begged him to make a batch of the Reali spaghetti recipe. It was an all-day process, so we always felt honored when he agreed to spend hours in the kitchen preparing it. What makes the Reali sauce unique is its pork rib base, which gives the sauce a richness and flavor unlike that of any other spaghetti sauce.

For years I would try to sneak a peek at the ingredients Larry was using when he was making his family treasured recipe, but he always knew I was watching and always managed to disguise precisely what he was putting into the sauce. When Larry paid a visit to Blue Heaven in 1969 armed with the ingredients to make a spaghetti dinner for the hunters, I purposely stayed in the shack that afternoon while the others went out to hunt and volunteered to assist him in preparing the famous Reali spaghetti sauce. He finally caved in and shared the secret of the family recipe with me. It is a recipe that needs to be shared with everyone who loves spaghetti as I do. It will serve at least 12 hungry people, and I always make a batch this size, as the leftover sauce freezes beautifully and can also be used for lasagna. Preparation time is about two hours.

Ingredients:

Olive oil

8-10 large cloves fresh garlic

4 large yellow onions

3 13.25-oz. cans mushrooms stems and pieces

4 12-oz. cans Contadina (or other "roma style") tomato paste

7 12-oz. cans water

2 tablespoons salt

2 teaspoons black pepper

6 tablespoons oregano flakes

3 tablespoons sweet basil flakes

4 large bay leaves

4 pounds venison hamburger or 80/20 ground beef

4 pounds pork ribs cut into 3-4" pieces

2 16-oz. packages of spaghetti

Romano or Parmesan cheese for garnish

Preparation:

You will need a large heavy-duty kettle with a lid in which to prepare the sauce. Always use low heat and stir the sauce frequently to keep the sauce from sticking and scorching on the bottom of the kettle.

Begin by putting a quarter-cup of olive oil in the kettle to help keep the sauce from sticking. Add the four 12-ounce cans of tomato paste to the kettle with seven 12-ounce cans of water and blend together. While that is slowly heating to a simmer on low heat, use a fry pan to brown the venison or ground beef seasoned with salt and pepper. Salt and pepper the pork ribs and slowly brown in a frying pan with a little olive oil or under the broiler. Once they're browned, drain the excess fat and add the hamburger and pork ribs to the kettle. Dice the four onions, sauté them in the fry pan with a little olive oil, and add them to the kettle. Drain the three cans of mushrooms and add them to the pot. Make certain that you frequently stir the sauce all the way to the bottom of the kettle. Peel the garlic cloves and either mince them or use a garlic press to add them to the sauce. Add the salt, pepper, oregano, basil, and bay leaves and blend them into the sauce. Simmer the sauce covered on low heat, stirring frequently. After about six hours, the ribs will separate from the rib bones. Pull the ribs from the sauce and place in a separate dish, checking the remaining sauce in the kettle for any stray rib bones and removing them. Cut up any large pieces of the pork ribs, return them to the pot, and continue to simmer for another hour or two. Usually, a dark-colored oil residue from the olive oil and ribs will appear at the top of the sauce after cooking for six to eight hours. This will be used to lubricate the pasta.

Serving:

About 45 minutes prior to serving, use a large kettle with salted water to boil the spaghetti according to package directions. I generally figure that one pound of spaghetti will serve about six people. When the spaghetti has been cooked "al dente," use a pasta strainer to drain the spaghetti of all water but do not rinse the spaghetti. Place the spaghetti back into the kettle. Skim the top of the spaghetti sauce and stir about two cups of it into the cooked spaghetti, blending the sauce into the spaghetti. This will keep the spaghetti from sticking together and will add another element of flavor to the finished dish. Serve the spaghetti by dishing the spaghetti with abundant sauce on top on individual plates, and leave the Romano or Parmesan cheese on the table for your guests to garnish as they please. Always warn your guests to be on the lookout for any stray rib bones.

Be prepared for your guests to ask for second or possibly even third helpings of your creation. It's that good! The Reali spaghetti is always complemented with toasted garlic bread and your favorite Italian salad and, of course, an ample supply of Merlot or your favorite red wine.

The hunters of Blue Heaven, along with a few camp guests, are shown enjoying the Reali spaghetti recipe, toasted garlic bread, Italian salad with anchovies and plenty of Merlot wine. Obviously, there is very little conversation that occurs during dinner as everyone is too busy cleaning their plates. (L-R) guest Daryl Salzman, R.D. Clagett (arm reaching for salt), Daryl's friend Steve Hauser, Ollie Hanson, Michael Schaaf, Brian Hanson, Barry Rice and guest Phillip Rasmussen. Ten of us gathered around the camp table that evening and consumed enormous quantities of spaghetti. No one walked away from the table hungry.

The Clagetts Arrive
Marriage of the Deer Camps

During deer season 1969 we had an unoccupied bunk, and Merle invited Dennis Clagett to join us for deer camp. Dennis had recently become Merle's son-in-law and had been a close friend of mine since 1965, when Dennis and I roomed together with several others in college. I was thrilled to have another younger hunter coming up for the hunt, as we needed more movement in the woods to push the deer onto one another. The Jolly Boys were getting older and although they still enjoyed their deer hunting, their enthusiasm for being in the woods for the entire day was obviously flagging. Most would rather have been back at the shack playing cribbage than sitting on their deer stands.

Dennis knew little about card-playing and had limited skills at the poker table, but he showed himself to be a skilled and patient hunter. During his first season with us, he shot a large doe on opening morning and followed later in the week by slaying a huge ten-point buck. His success that year begat friendly competition between the two of us in each succeeding year, and we competed to see who could shoot the biggest buck. Merle's son, John Kimball, also shot his first buck that season, and we considered the hunt to be very fruitful, considering the limited number of deer in our area that year.

My father penned an entry in the camp log at the end of the season which simply summarized the season:

> *"1969 hunting season commenced Nov. 22nd - Present 1st weekend were Marv, John H., Bob H., Merle, John D., Dennis Clagett, Adder, Phillip - Had T-bones Sat. nite – Ken Sugrue came up to join us Sunday nite to go to Camp No-Hunt. Dennis killed nice doe 1st Sat. for camp meat. John Kimball killed his 1st buck Sunday. Fork horn - Dennis killed 10 point buck Tues. Merle, Marv and Dennis dragged it through the north swamp until after dark. We three and wives stayed overnight. Merle & Marv stayed Wed. nite. Dennis, John H., John D., Larry Reali, Marv, Merle & Adder came out the last Friday night. Larry made spaghetti – very good – very good season – let's do it again."*

Dennis possessed excellent mechanical and electronic skills, and his expertise in keeping the light plant running smoothly was immediately utilized by the Jolly Boys, who had struggled with the light plant for years.

In previous years Dennis had hunted with his father, Russell, as well as another father-son duo in the "Hungry Run" area of eastern

Sawyer County. It was rugged terrain, and there wasn't a hunting shack available to them. He informed us that they would enter the woods before daylight and would hunt until noon. They would then start a small fire to warm up and toast cheese sandwiches over the fire for their lunch. Usually, the bread ended up burned and the cheese remained frozen from being carried in their pockets all morning. It was the way that they had always hunted. They would put out their fire and then hunt until dark to return home, cold and tired. Naturally, Dennis fell in love with Blue Heaven and the way the Jolly Boys ran their deer camp, so much so that the following year, Dennis asked the Jolly Boys for their permission to invite his father up to experience Blue Heaven.

Well known in the Hayward area, Russell Clagett and his wife, Betty, co-owned and operated Herman's Landing on the Chippewa Flowage with another couple. Russ was an avid sportsman and an icon in the Hayward resort community. We all thought that he would easily fit in with the rest of us at Blue Heaven. Dennis and Russ arrived on the Sunday night of the first weekend of the 1970 season, after the rest of us had already been in camp for a couple of days. The two of them decided that even though it was already dark, they would walk in carrying their gear rather than pester any of the Jolly Boys to provide transportation. Camp No-Hunt was already there for the annual Sunday night party, and the small hunting shack was full of hunters. The party was in full swing when they arrived, and both of them immediately joined in the merriment and the spirit of the evening.

The Jolly Boys had decided that this year would be the year that the two camps should "become wed" to signify the bond that they had developed. The Jolly Boys took Carl Benson, who was the patriarch of Camp No-Hunt, back into the bunk area and dressed him in an old wedding gown, complete with a pillow stuffed into the front of the dress so Carl looked as though he were about nine months pregnant. Carl was the "bride," and Kenny Sugrue, our beloved mayor of Hayward, represented the Jolly Boys as the groom. Merle dressed up as the minister and performed the ceremony at an altar he had thrown together with linens and candles. Adder had the honor of being best man for the groom, and a friend of Carl's was Carl's maid of honor. By the time the ceremony ended, there wasn't a dry eye in the place, not from tears of joy or sadness, but from tears of laughter.

Russell, like Dennis, was a perfect fit in our hunting camp. That deer season formed a relationship that would last twenty-eight years.

(L-R) Merle serving as minister, a friend of Carl's as bridesmaid, Carl'ine' Benson as the bride, Ken Sugrue as the groom and Adder serving as best man.

The ceremony concluded, the celebration began with photos and best wishes. (L-R) Marv Hanson, Carl's friend, Carl Benson, Ken Sugrue and Vern Inhoff.

The Chili Feeds

During the early years of the hunting shack, it was a challenge for the Jolly Boys and the other hunters in our camp to break away early on the Friday before deer season. Frequently, no one was available to leave for Blue Heaven until late Friday afternoon. As the years passed and vacation time became more available, the majority of hunters in our camp were able to time it so they would be available by late Friday morning. That was when my mother's chili feed tradition began, one year in the early 1970s.

My parents had the ideal home to entertain a large group of guests. Built in 1910, it had a large kitchen and attached pantry, and the dining room table sat 12 people. It became the common meeting place for everyone to assemble, and my mother volunteered to serve a noon lunch of chili to all of the hunters before they left for camp. It was always a festive gathering, and the anticipation of the hunt was in the air. My father would be at the grocery store, gathering supplies for the deer camp, and several of the hunters would show up as early as mid-morning to handle the other chores, knowing that my mother always had the coffee pot on and tins of delicious cookies sitting out on her kitchen table. When my father came home around noon, she would begin to dish the chili and serve it to the hunters seated at the dining room table. Several of the hunters' wives were there to assist her. There were always large bowls of saltine crackers, toasted garlic bread with butter, and milk or beer to wash everything down. Cookies were for dessert. Almost everyone had a second helping of chili, and some even had three bowls.

The tradition of the chili feed at my mother's continued until she passed away in 2003. To this day, we still hold the tradition of the pre-deer season chili feed, but we now have it up at camp on the Friday noon before deer season. We still use my mother's recipe for the chili.

VIOLET'S CHILI

3 lbs. venison hamburger (80/20 ground beef if venison hamburger isn't available)
2 large yellow onions, chopped
2 cups celery, chopped
1 46-oz. V-8 juice
2 28-oz. cans crushed tomatoes
2 16-oz. cans dark red kidney beans
1 16-oz. can light red kidney beans
1 13.25-oz. can mushrooms stems & pieces
Tablespoon of salt, tablespoon of pepper
2 tablespoons of chili powder

Brown hamburger and add onion and celery as hamburger is cooking. Drain excess fat. Add V-8 juice and crushed tomatoes. Drain and add kidney beans and mushrooms; add salt, pepper, and chili powder. Simmer on low heat for three hours. Serve with saltines and butter and put chili powder on the table for those wanting additional heat. Chili can be garnished with sprinkles of chopped raw onion, shredded cheddar cheese, and Fritos if desired.

The 1970s

When I read through all the entries in the shack log from the decade of the 1970s, I am constantly reminded of the importance of the shack log, which provides a diary and chronological history of the memories and events that have taken place at Blue Heaven year after year. The log was always kept on a shelf and available for anyone in camp to make an entry or just read the contents of the log for their entertainment. It wasn't at all unusual to see one of the hunters reading through the log late at night by candlelight or early in the morning while sipping on a cup of coffee. They would always have a little smile on their face while they were reading, reminiscing about the many good times recorded in the log, which was becoming tattered from use.

There are multiple entries in the log relating tales of the deer hunt or just coming up to the shack in the dead of winter while putting up with sub-zero temperatures or knee-high snow. There are stories of New Year's Eve parties with family and friends; fall and spring frolic parties; snowmobiling and cross-country skiing parties; and trips in the fall and spring to cut wood, make improvements or repairs, or fight the never-ending battles to control the mice or porcupines that didn't want to seem to leave the place alone when we weren't there to protect it. The log always reflected who was there during an event and leaves one with the impression that a substantial number of people from the Hayward area honored the Jolly Boys with a visit to Blue Heaven at one time or another.

The decade of the '70s was a period that produced very few deer for the Jolly Boys and the other hunters at Blue Heaven. Even though few deer were taken in each of those seasons, it didn't seem to matter much. As long as one or two deer were slain, everyone seemed happy that we would be able to enjoy venison for the deer season, even if there wasn't much left over to take home to stock our freezers. Party-deer tags were being offered through those years, and even though the Jolly Boys managed to get their share of the permits, there were many seasons when they went unfilled.

On 11/17/1973, there is an entry in the log which states that I

> *"killed a 9 point buck and a doe 200 yards east of 'The Can'. Temperature in mid-30's with tracking snow on ground. Merle prepared a pork roast with dressing, squash, salad and mashed potatoes for dinner after a great poker game and happy hour."*

I vividly recall that opening Saturday of deer season, because after I was lucky enough to shoot those two deer, I was dressing them out and could hear a pack of coyotes howling about 200 yards north of me. Naturally I was concerned that after I left the area to get the Coot to haul the deer back to camp, the coyotes would move in and devour the deer. I double-timed it back to the shack to find someone to help me load up the deer and bring them back to the shack. The only hunter in camp was Adder. He was in his mid-sixties at that time, and although he wanted to help, he felt that it was beyond his capabilities to do so. I recall how bad I felt for him as he stood there and apologized for not being able to provide any assistance to me. It was there and then that I came to the realization that the Jolly Boys were starting to age, and I knew that it was just a matter of time when Blue Heaven would be a camp of older hunters more apt to stay in the shack and play cribbage than tramp the woods looking for deer.

On February 3, 1975, Kenny Sugrue, the beloved Jolly Boy with the golden singing voice, passed away. The Jolly Boys were now only three, and I became aware that there would be many changes ahead for Blue Heaven in the coming years.

1980

During the summer and fall of 1980, loggers moved into the woods around Blue Heaven to harvest basswood. The tree farmers with their huge wheels had made a complete mess of all the logging roads in the area, leaving big ruts which quickly filled with water and became mud holes. The Jolly Boys were concerned about transportation to the shack, come deer season, and were hoping for an early freeze that year.

Deer season arrived, and there was very little snow on the ground, with the temperatures in the mid-thirties. The road was still a mess. If it hadn't been for the Coot, we would have had no choice but to haul in all of our supplies and gear by hand, as the road into camp was impassable. We had only six in camp for that opening weekend. My father and I, Merle and JK Dunster, and Dennis and Russ Clagett were in attendance. Adder wasn't there that year for deer season, and there were only two of the five original Jolly Boys occupying their bunks. It seemed unusual to have only six of us there for the opening weekend, because in prior years most of the bunks had been filled. At the end of the first weekend, the Jolly Boys granted permission for my oldest son Robin to come up to hunt. He was thirteen, a part of the future for Blue Heaven, and his being a part of the group was just as important to his grandfather and me as it was to him. There were now three generations of Hansons occupying bunks at Blue Heaven and the pride on my father's face was very evident.

Rob had been up at Blue Heaven on countless occasions previously, but this was the first time he was allowed to come into deer camp, carry a rifle, and hunt. Although he managed to see a deer and get a shot off at it, he unfortunately missed it. I knew he was disappointed, but he took it in stride. Wanting him to get the full flavor of being a part of hunting shack life, my father and I staked him a few dollars so he could participate in the evening poker games. Although he managed to win a couple of hands, it wasn't too long before the rest of the players had all of his money on their side

My older son, Robin, thrilled to win his first poker game at Blue Heaven.

of the table. We all knew that in future seasons, experience and seasoning would make him a great deer hunter and poker player.

The following fall we decided it was time to replace the outhouse that had served us well for over 25 years. The old outhouse was rotting at the base, and it was just a matter of time before it toppled over. One of my friends, Dennis Skare, volunteered to donate an old outhouse that he had out at his lake cabin, and we quickly took him up on the offer. It wasn't in the best condition, but it still had many years of serviceable life left. We loaded it up on the back of my pickup to transport it the twenty miles up to Blue Heaven. Naturally, en route to the shack, we had to drive up and down the main street of Hayward a couple of times to show off our cargo. When we arrived at the road leading in to the shack, I put my truck into 4-wheel drive and began to churn our way through the mud holes with our heavy load. About a hundred yards before reaching the shack, there is one particularly nasty mud hole to be maneuvered which is about fifty yards long. Anticipating that we might mire down in the middle of it, I greatly increased our speed and entered the mud hole going as fast as we could, hoping that I would be able to maintain control of the truck and avoid getting stuck. To my delight and amazement, we made it to the other side, chugged up the small hill, and arrived at the shack. We got out of the truck and discovered that the outhouse was no longer on the back of the pickup. It was lying back in that nasty mud hole. We had been too attentive trying to make it through the mud hole to know it had bounced off. After the laughter died down and with a lot of effort, we were able to retrieve the outhouse from the mud hole and get it up to the shack.

Fortunately, the mishap didn't cause much damage to the little building, and the Skare outhouse is still in service at Blue Heaven.

1981

During the summer months of 1981, the loggers that had been in our area returned with their trucks to haul out the rest of the logs they had cut and used a bulldozer to smooth out most of the logging road leading to our shack. Even the big logging trucks couldn't maneuver through the mud holes that had been created by their tree farmers. Although the road was still in tough shape, we were thrilled to see the improvements, with most of the huge ruts being smoothed over.

Starting In 1980, the Wisconsin DNR felt that the deer herd was expanding to a point where they began to issue "hunter's choice" permits. We also called them "either-sex" permits, as it allowed the hunter fortunate enough to get the permit to shoot either a buck or a doe. If you had the permit, you didn't have to determine if the deer had horns or not before you started shooting. We didn't obtain the coveted permit in 1980, but during the deer season of 1981, Russ and I both obtained a hunter's choice permit. On opening morning, Rob shot at a spike buck but missed it. Later that day, the spike buck came by my stand, and I was more fortunate, managing to bring it down. I collected $8.00 off the deer horns for getting the "first set of nuts," and we tagged the deer with a tag from one of the older hunters in our camp. The following day, Russ filled his either-sex permit by shooting a huge doe, and Dennis also came dragging a nice six-point buck into camp. We had three deer hanging by the end of opening weekend and rejoiced in the fact that the deer population in our area seemed to be improving.

Not to be outdone for the season by my friend Dennis, I shot an eight-point buck a couple of days later. On the Wednesday morning of that season, it had started snowing quite heavily just as we were all returning to the shack for our noon brunch. By the time we were done eating, there were already several inches of new heavy, wet snow on the ground. We were all eager to get back into the woods for the afternoon hunt. I decided that I would walk down a new access road that the loggers had made which went through an area of thick tag alders and aspen saplings. I figured that if I were a deer, that area was one I would want to be in for shelter when it was snowing heavily. As I began my trek down that road, I marveled at the silence of the snowfall. There was no wind. The air was wet, making it difficult for a deer to smell you, and you could sneak down that road in complete silence. These were ideal hunting conditions, and I thought that I had a good chance of sneaking up on a deer during this snowstorm. I soon came across a huge track in the snow of a deer that had recently crossed the road. There was only a small amount of new snow in the track, so I decided to follow it. I was only about 30 yards away from the road in the thickness of the tag alders when I came across a deer bed that was so fresh that there was hardly any of the new snow lying in it. My heart started to beat heavily in my chest as I once again started to follow the fresh deer tracks, taking one small step at a time and making every effort to move in complete silence. I knew I was close to this deer. I had walked only about 20 yards, and there, looking at me through the tag alders and the freshly falling snow, was a magnificent buck staring directly at me. He seemed to be confused, wondering how I had gotten that close to him without his hearing or smelling me. I slowly raised my rifle to my shoulder, took careful aim at the thickest part of his neck, and fired. He immediately whirled around and began running through the thick underbrush. I rushed over to where he had been standing and found blood and deer hair lying on top of the snow. I knew I had hit him but didn't know how badly he was hit. I then did something that I had never done before and have never done since. Normally, I would have waited for a bit to follow a wounded deer before I began to track him so he would bed down. However, I was worried, as he was heading towards an area where hunters from another deer camp had their stands, so I started running after that deer. Although I was 37 years old, the adrenaline must have been flowing, as I was leaping over windfalls and was at a dead run with my rifle at "port-arms" attempting to catch up with him. As soon as I got through the tag alders in an area where the woods opened up into an area of large basswoods, I stopped and could see him standing broadside to me about a hundred yards away, trying to determine if I was still following him. I raised my rifle and emptied it in his direction, and he went down. I ran over to him and saw that he was a huge animal and had a magnificent eight point rack. I field-dressed him, attached my deer tag, and returned to camp to summon help to get him back to the shack.

1982-1983

No one can explain why but there are no entries in the shack log for the deer seasons of 1982 and 1983. My father wrote a note in the log,

> *"Camp operated each season but nobody recorded '82 & '83. Shack damaged by falling trees 7/3/83 and in fall of '83 we did a lot of work cleaning roads, repairing shack and installing new roof. Three deer taken in 1983."*

In looking at the shade we have which records all of the deer kills, it shows that I shot a six-point buck and a doe in 1982 and that we shot two deer in 1983. Using my hunter's choice tag, I shot a doe, and Robin shot his first deer that year: a spike buck.

On 7/3/83, straight-line winds went through the area of our hunting camp, changing the landscape and the way we would hunt for many years to come. The "golden land" of maples around the shack was gone forever and the road leading in to the shack was clogged with trees covering the road. They estimated that the winds had been about 80 mph, and it looked as if an atomic bomb had exploded in the area. Nothing was spared, and there were very few mature trees left standing. The landmarks in the area were no longer recognizable, and we knew a huge task was ahead of us just to cut our way in to the hunting shack to see if it had survived this devastating storm. The weekend after the storm hit, we all gathered in force at the road and began to cut our way in. Everyone showed up for this event, armed with chain saws and a goal that we cut a trail on the road in to the shack before nightfall. It was hot, and the mosquitoes and deer flies were in abundance. Cutting the debris off the road was no easy chore. The wind had come from the west, and the first portion of the road leading into the shack ran in a southerly direction, so all of the trees were lying fully across the road. The windstorm had been so violent that the trees were intertwined; when they were cut, they often acted as if they were spring-loaded, so that one had to be extremely careful while cutting. It was a slow, tedious process, but by noon we were halfway there, having cut a path through the debris just wide enough for the Coot to pass through. After a short lunch break, we went back to the task at hand and finally arrived at the shack late that afternoon.

We were all tired and wet with sweat but were completely relieved to find that although the entire area around the building had been devastated, Blue Heaven and the three small out-buildings had been spared. A large basswood immediately next to the entry door had broken off about midway down its thirty- foot height, and the top of the tree had clipped off a corner of the roof, but everything else was intact. The top of the tree was still lying on the roof, which meant that it would be a challenge to slide it off without creating further damage, but we thought we could accomplish that. The chimney to the wood stove was also broken, but that could be replaced. So much debris had hit the shingles that the roofing was shattered and would need replacement. All in all, we thought that it could have been much worse, as one of the fallen trees could have easily demolished any of the buildings. We returned to the shack on numerous weekends thereafter, building a ramp to slide the basswood off the shack roof, repairing the damages, and attempting to get the camp ready for the upcoming deer season.

When deer season 1983 arrived, we all knew that it would be a difficult hunt due to the thousands of trees that had been blown over in the area. We frequently spoke about staying at Blue Heaven at night but going out of the area during the day to hunt for deer. On opening morning, we all left camp, trying to reach our favorite hunting stands. It was almost an impossible mission, as one had to crawl over, crawl under, or find a way around all the trees that were blocking the normal routes to the hunting stands. We also questioned whether any deer were still in the area and believed that many of them might have gone elsewhere.

Robin was now 16 years old and decided he would try to make his way down Birch Street to see if he could find any deer sign in the area. I was still at the shack loading my rifle to leave on the hunt when I heard him shoot numerous times. There was a pause, and then more gunfire. Another pause, and then a couple more shots. I started heading in his direction, figuring that he wasn't more than a couple hundred yards away from the shack. As I began crawling over, under, and on the fallen trees, I heard him yelling, "Dad! Dad!! Dad!!!"

Fearing the worse, I moved towards him as quickly as possible and finally saw him standing in a hollow by a small creek. It appeared as if there was a deer lying on the ground next to him. I finally reached him and asked what was wrong. I could see that the deer was mortally wounded but still alive. He responded, "I ran out of bullets!" He had shot a spike buck but had run out of ammunition with which to finish the job. I quickly gave the deer a coup de gras shot to put it out of its misery. He was thrilled to have shot his first buck.

The remainder of the season was spent trying to locate old landmarks and deer stands that were now no longer recognizable due to all of the storm debris. I managed to shoot a doe later in the season near the shack, but no other deer were seen that year. It was if all of us were trying to hunt in a foreign land.

The three-quarter mile road into the shack was intertwined with fallen trees that would snap and spring like slingshots when they were being cut.

We finally cut our way into Blue Heaven and found the shack still standing even though it was covered with trees that had fallen all around it.

A large basswood was broken but was caught up in another tree before it could demolish the shack. The southeast corner of the roof had been ripped off by a branch.

Our hunting area at the start of deer season 1983 was total devastation from the straight-line winds that had blown through the area that summer.

1984-1986

The next several years following the huge windstorm of 1983 would be spent trying to reclaim our hunting area around Blue Heaven. Whenever we went up to the shack during that time, we would have a work party and make an effort to cut open another trail to make it easier to reach one of our favorite deer stands. We knew that it was just a matter of time before loggers would come in to the area to harvest all of the downed timber, but until that time came, we had to depend on our own resources to make it possible to hunt near our deer camp.

My father wrote in the log on 11/17/84:

"Arrived Friday the 16th for deer season. All settled by 4 p.m. and Marv, John H., Bob H., J. K., Merle, Russ, Dennis and Adder in attendance. Merle killed 6 point buck 1st day but nothing else all season. We did not have any either-sex permits this year. Weather all season outstanding but hunting was poor. Woods are desolate due to the big blow of 7/3/83 but we all had a great time."

The log records in subsequent years go on to reflect all the efforts that the Jolly Boys extended attempting to clear out their hunting grounds and return them to some degree of normal. If deer were in the area, they were difficult to see, and making a drive to push them anywhere was still out of the question. In 1985, heavy snow complicated the deer season, and we only shot one doe even though we had several hunter's choice permits.

The year 1986 presented quite a scare to the Jolly Boys. There was a movement by the county to possibly eliminate the recreational use permits for deer camps, and a large meeting was held by the county board to invite public input. There were only two other counties in Wisconsin that were still granting the permits. Both my father and Adder attended the meeting, along with a multitude of others who held the permits for deer camps. My father was quoted in the Sawyer County Record newspaper as addressing the county board and stating, *"I have gone to hunting camps since I was a kid and we have a tradition. My son killed his first buck at our camp and his son did too. We searched for wild land to buy to build our deer camp and believe me, there isn't much available."* He also argued that the county needed to promote hunting in the area, and the camp permits were allowing that to be accomplished. Adder also addressed the county board, saying, *"We think it's a great privilege to have this right for a camp on county property and to be able to hunt on it. We don't complain about the fee."*

The fee for the recreational use permit at that time was only $50 per year. Shortly after this meeting, the fee was raised to $100 per year, which was still a bargain in the eyes of the Jolly Boys. They had been hunting on this area of county property for over 30 years at this point and didn't want to have to move their camp off county land. Ultimately, the county board decided to extend the recreational use permits to the present holders of the permits but also wanted to start a 25-year phase-out of the permits, similar to the policy of other neighboring counties. This issue of terminating the recreational use permits would continue to be a topic of discussion in the years to come.

That deer season my younger son, Oliver, came to deer camp. He had turned 14 and was now allowed to come up to hunt with the Jolly Boys. Ollie had been waiting for his opportunity to be up at the shack with his grandpa, dad, and brother and spent that entire season tramping every square inch of the woods around our deer camp looking for deer. Although he did not find success his first year at the shack, there was no doubt in anyone's mind about his enthusiasm for the hunt.

Hunting conditions improved slightly in 1986 and 1987, and we were able to harvest three deer in each of those two seasons. We were also seeing more deer sign in the area, and saplings were springing up in the blown-down tree debris, giving the deer more food and shelter. My father was entering his 70s, and it was obvious that standing next to that old wood cook stove preparing the meals at camp was taking its toll on him. It was getting time for him to kick back and sit at the table, play cribbage, and allow someone else to do the grunt work of cooking. He had always been the head chef at Blue Heaven. Merle would help out on occasion, but my father had always done the planning, the grocery-shopping, and the cooking for our group. I told him that it was time for him to step down and that I would take over for him. He didn't argue.

My father excelled with almost all of the menu items that we dined on at camp. One exception was fried eggs, which the hunters in our camp called "snotty eggs." He would always fry the eggs in gobs of butter in the huge cast-iron skillet that we also used for frying venison. The eggs would be served directly from the skillet to the plates on the table sitting in front of the hunters. He would always grab an egg or two with the spatula and then ask the hunter, "How do you want your eggs?" No one ever responded, because the eggs were always cooked the same way, slightly singed on the bottom and totally undercooked on the top. My first priority was to serve properly cooked fried eggs. To accomplish that task, I purchased a large non-stick fry pan and brought it up to the shack. I put in a small pat of butter, allowed it to melt, got the fry pan hot, and cracked the eggs into the fry pan. I would then add about a tablespoon of water to the pan and put a tight lid on it so the tops of the eggs would steam while they were frying on medium heat. The eggs always turned out perfectly cooked. The whites of the eggs were perfection, and the yolks were always creamy and ready to be broken with a piece of toast. It was obvious that everyone was thrilled to be finally getting properly cooked eggs, and although a few joked that they missed my dad's "snotty eggs," we always knew that they were kidding.

My youngest son, Oliver "Ollie" Hanson, started hunting in 1986 at age 14 and hasn't missed a deer season since. His Grandfather, Jolly Boy Marvin Hanson, beamed with pride that he now had his son and two of his grandsons as part of the Blue Heaven deer camp.

A favorite brunch item is properly fried eggs, pancakes smothered in butter and maple syrup with home-made jelly or jam and venison breakfast sausage.

Another brunch favorite is omelets made with eggs, cheddar cheese, chopped and sautéed bacon, onions, red pepper and mushrooms with a fry pan full of potatoes and onions fried in butter and laced with pork sausage or diced ham.

Ribs and Kraut

My father was aware that I knew my way around the kitchen. I had been taught how to cook by my mother in my early teens when both of my parents were working late hours in their grocery store. My sister didn't like to cook, so my mother would call me from work, inform me of the menu for the evening meal, and then guide me through the preparation step by step. I was soon doing chicken, pot roast, and similar dinners with ease.

We have a number of favorites that we dine on the first weekend of deer camp. Second only to the Reali spaghetti that is served, pork ribs with sauerkraut is requested by everyone each year. Properly prepared, it is probably the best of comfort foods. Improperly prepared, it can be disastrous, possibly even painful.

My father started serving ribs and kraut the first Saturday night on the opening weekend every year at Blue Heaven in the early sixties. He would purchase pork ribs and sauerkraut, place everything in a roasting pan with a tight lid on it, and allowed it to slow cook in the oven of the wood burning cook stove for about three hours until the ribs were falling off the bone. He used what he lovingly referred to as his "rotation method." This involved pulling the roaster out of the oven about every half hour or so, rotating the roaster 180 degrees so all the ingredients would turn upside down, and then sliding it back into the oven for further cooking. This always turned out delicious and was served over buttered baked potatoes with generous amounts of salt and pepper. Everyone always raved, and enormous quantities were consumed by the hungry hunters.

There was one minor problem. Most of the hunters in the camp would end up with various degrees of lower intestinal distress shortly after dinner. The outhouse would be in constant demand throughout the evening and the early morning hours. It didn't take a rocket scientist to figure out that consuming the grease from the pork ribs and the brine from the sauerkraut might not be a good thing for the body. It had the same effect as a strong laxative.

After a number of years of this abuse, I pleaded with my father to allow me to cook the ribs and kraut. After much debate, he finally gave in and allowed me to try my skill at preparing this popular dish. The first thing I did was to render the fat off the ribs by precooking them in the oven until they turned brown. This eliminated much of all that nasty fat within the meat. I also purchased the sauerkraut in plastic bags rather than in cans or jars. This allowed me to snip the top of the bag and squeeze out the majority of the brine from the sauerkraut. I then took things one step further and fried the kraut in a frying pan with a little butter to steam off any remaining brine. The ribs were put in a large roasting pan with the sauerkraut on the top of the ribs, and the roasting pan was covered with a tight layer of aluminum foil to seal in all the juices while everything slow- roasted. Amazingly enough, my method of cooking this dish was equal to what my father had previously prepared for several years, with one exception: no one got sick. You will love this recipe.

RIBS AND KRAUT

Ingredients:
Purchase either pork ribs or country-style pork ribs. Buy ribs that are meaty but not overly lean for the best flavor. Figure on one pound of ribs per person.

Purchase the sauerkraut in the 32-oz. plastic bags rather than in cans or jars so the brine can be easily squeezed out. Figure on one bag of kraut for every three people.

Salt – pepper – butter or margarine

Preparation:
Cut the pork ribs into serving-sized pieces about three to four inches wide. If you're using country-style ribs, there is no need to do anything. Place the pork on a broiling pan and liberally salt and pepper both sides of the pork. Put the pork into a 400-degree oven or under the broiler and broil both sides of the pork until they start to turn brown but do not overcook. Discard fat and put the pork into a deep roasting pan.

Snip the top of the sauerkraut bags and squeeze them to remove the brine. Remove the sauerkraut from the bags and put it into a non-stick frying pan with about three tablespoons of butter or margarine. Slowly fry the sauerkraut on medium heat until it starts to brown but do not overcook. Remove the sauerkraut from the frying pan and place it on top of the ribs.

Cover the top of the roaster with aluminum foil to make an airtight seal. Preheat oven to 325 degrees and cook for two and one-half to three hours until the top of the sauerkraut is a golden brown and the ribs fall apart with the touch of a fork.

Serve with baked potatoes that can be baked while the ribs and kraut are baking. Cut potatoes open and butter them heavily, adding salt and pepper to taste. This is best served with the sauerkraut on top of the baked potato and the ribs to the side.

A roaster full of falling-off-the-bone pork spareribs and sauerkraut with a bowl of "shack-baked potatoes" sitting in the center of the table on a cutting board await a group of hungry hunters. Definitely comfort food at its best.

SHACK GREEN BEANS WITH VINEGAR, ONION, AND BACON

In late February of 1987, my parents, Dennis, Ollie, and I went up to the shack to spend Saturday night just to relax, play some cards, and have a good venison dinner. There was enough snow on the ground for snowmobiling, and we had just settled in when we saw two snowmobilers coming up the trail towards the shack. They stopped and removed their helmets. It was Chuck and his daughter Stephanie from Nelson Lake Landing. My parents knew them well, as they would often stop at Chuck's resort for a hamburger and pitcher of beer. Chuck's wife, Linda, was in California visiting her parents, and my father immediately extended an invitation for Chuck and his daughter to join us for a venison fry that evening. Chuck readily accepted but only on the condition that they could contribute to the dinner. Unknown to us, Chuck gathered wild mushrooms every fall, and he insisted that I go over to the resort and bring back several packages he had in his freezer to go with the venison steak. Our dinner that evening was one to remember. Fried venison tenderloins with Chuck's sautéed wild mushrooms, shack baked potatoes, and a shack dish my dad had invented called shack green beans. Shack green beans complement a variety of main dishes and have somewhat of a German flair to them, as they are cooked with vinegar, onion, and bacon.

SHACK GREEN BEANS

This is very simple to put together and will serve 6 to 8 people. Take one pound of bacon, slice it into one-inch cubes, and fry it in a large frying pan until it is very crispy. Remove the bacon pieces from the bacon fat and place on a paper towel to drain. Using the bacon grease in the frying pan, sauté one whole onion that has been peeled and diced into large pieces until the onion is tender and transparent. Drain the bacon grease off the onion. Drain three 14.5-ounce cans of cut green beans and put in the frying pan with the onion. Add the bacon and about two cups of red wine vinegar. Liberally salt and pepper and simmer everything until all of the vinegar evaporates.

1987-1989

The decade of the 1980's wound down without much excitement or fanfare up at the hunting shack. In 1987, Dennis shot a very nice eight-point buck, and I shot a small buck and a doe. We had three either-sex permits that year, and two of them went unfilled. The following year we also had three either-sex permits, and none of them got filled. It was almost a season where we got skunked until I managed to shoot a small four-pointer, but by that time it was too late in the season to cut up the deer for our table. We were without venison but still ate well. We dined on meatloaf on the first Friday night, followed by spaghetti for Saturday and a wonderful pork roast with all of the trimmings on Sunday. Monday night we had to settle for leftover spaghetti, and on Tuesday we dined on the leftover pork roast. It was almost embarrassing that we were at deer camp and didn't have venison to enjoy, but we made it through the remainder of the season dining on ribs and kraut and a pot roast done to perfection with potatoes and carrots. We also had lots of leftover turkey from Thanksgiving, so we made do without venison that year.

In the fall of 1989, we organized a work party to finish cutting a trail through the storm debris of 1983 up to "the Can" on north lane. Even though it had been six years since the straight-line winds, much of our hunting area remained a mess. With the completion of this project, we finally felt as if most of our hunting area had been reclaimed.

Deer season 1989 turned out to be very successful. There were a couple of inches of snow on the ground, and we had five hunter's-choice permits between the eight of us in camp. We had an open bunk, and I had received permission from the Jolly Boys to invite a friend by the name of Randy Stuggen up from Milwaukee for the opening weekend. My dad, Adder, Russ, and Uncle Bobby were getting up there in age, so Dennis and I welcomed a younger hunter to join the two of us to push the deer around. Although we saw lots of deer tracks and sign in the area on opening day, no one saw any deer.

Sunday was much better. I had found a place to sit early that morning on a stand we had named the " the Ravine," which is high on a hill in the hardwoods overlooking a tag alder swamp. I had just settled in and was optimistic that a deer would be walking along the edge of that swamp at any moment. I had been sitting there for about 15 minutes and was starting to do some serious daydreaming when a deer stood up from behind a windfall about a hundred yards away down by the tag alders. The deer apparently hadn't heard me walking into my stand but had gotten a smell of me once I had settled in. He didn't see me but I saw him. I put my scope on the deer and could see it was a spike buck. One shot, and the deer went down in the bed from which he had risen. At noon on that day, Dennis connected with an eight-point buck several hundred yards north of where I had been sitting that morning. Dennis got turned around after he dressed the deer and headed back to camp, and we had a tough time finding that deer later that afternoon. We had an even more difficult time dragging the deer through several swamps to get to a location where we could transport it back to the shack, using the Coot. We had two bucks hanging, and everyone was chomping at the bit to return to the woods the next morning for more action.

Monday turned out to be even more exciting than Sunday. I was walking on a deer trail next to the swamp towards the stand we call the Big Rock when a herd of deer came running directly at me. There were two bucks and three does. My attention went first to the biggest buck, which had a five-point rack. I dropped him after two shots. I then fired three shots at the smaller buck that had eight-inch spike antlers, and he went down. I immediately changed clips in my rifle and started shooting at the does that were running up a hill away from all the commotion. I managed to get one, but the other two made their escape. A few moments later, both Randy and my Uncle Bob, who had heard all of the shots, showed up at my location. Randy had never dressed a deer before, so I was able to show him how it was done; he then took over and dressed out the other two deer. My uncle had already started back to the shack to summon transportation and to spread the news that I had three deer lying in the woods.

We took it easy for the remainder of that deer season. When it came time to break camp, we had five deer hanging from the deer pole and felt we had plenty of venison to share with everyone. That year, 1989, had been a great year for Wisconsin deer hunters. There had been 661,713 licenses sold and 310,192 deer registered.

1990

There is an entry in the log dated 10/20/1990 which reads,

> *"Work party consisting of Marv, John, Robin, Russ, Dennis & Bob arrive to open camp & prepare for deer season. Split wood & cut more yellow birch for next season. Russell had volunteered to bring venison tenderloins for supper, but the package turned out to be a large venison shank roast! Made do with making shack steak out of the shank roast and added some hamburger to it and served it over mashed potatoes. Russell is depressed and drinks more than his average share of gin and winds up trying to crawl into Bobby's bunk at bedtime. Marvin doesn't tolerate that type of activity and makes Russ return to his own bunk."*

Lesson learned: always label your wrapped meat before throwing it into the freezer.

Deer season 1990 was a bust but we still had a lot of fun. We had seven hunter's-choice permits between us and all nine bunks were full, but the weather wasn't cooperating. There was no snow, and record highs were being registered, with temperatures rising into the high sixties each day. On opening morning Rob managed to shoot a doe, but the rest of the deer tags went unfilled that season because it was impossible to tell where the deer were in the area without any snow on the ground. The highlights of that season came in the form of humor. Russ related that he had been hunting and "nature called" in the middle of his hunt. Like most hunters, he simply dropped his pants, and took care of his business. He redressed, began to continue on his hunt, and fell flat on his face. It appears that when he pulled his hunting pants back up, he neglected to pull up his long johns, so they got tangled around his ankles, causing him to trip. He was happy no one had been around to witness the event. Not to be outdone, my father reported that he had been walking down a hill and slipped on some leaves. He fell to the ground and couldn't get back up on his feet no matter how hard he shoved with his hand. It turns out that my dad had been trying to shove himself up while he had his hand on his "heater-seater" clipped to the back of the belt on his pants. He was also happy no one had been around to witness the event.

Adder's Ladder

After Adder turned 79, we all noticed that he was having difficulty getting in and out of his bunk, which was the center one between my father's and Merle's. Although a chair was there to use as a stepping stool, Adder was not a tall man, and his bunk was almost five feet off the floor. It was difficult for a man his age to maneuver in and out of that center bunk, and we all knew that he would not be comfortable in a lower bunk where it got too cold during the night. All of us were concerned that he might have an accident in the middle of the night in the event he tried to get out of his bunk.

I looked around in my garage at home, found some scrap two-by-twelves and constructed Adder a twelve-inch-wide stairway to reach from the floor to the top of his bunk. I took a black magic marker, wrote "Adder's Ladder" on it, and brought the stairway up with me for the 1990 deer season.

I must admit that I had some misgivings about presenting that ladder as a gift to Adder. I certainly didn't want to insult him. I slid the stairway into the shack and laid it on the floor, explaining its function to Adder. To my delight, he was thrilled. We immediately installed it next to his bunk, and he used it for several years after to get in and out of his bunk. He even brought up pieces of scrap carpeting to install on the steps to prevent the possibility of getting any slivers in his bare feet.

"SNOWDIN"

The hunters at Blue Heaven often speculated what a thrill it would be to be snowed in at the hunting shack during deer season. It would be great fun to be stranded deep in the woods with ample food and drink, riding out a major winter storm, with no place to go and nothing to do except "deal the cards"! As the old saying goes, "Be careful what you wish for."

The autumn of 1991 had been beautiful. We spent several weekends preparing the hunting camp for the upcoming deer season scheduled to begin on November 23. On October 31, a major winter storm cranked up and swept through northwestern Wisconsin, depositing up to thirty inches of heavy, wet snow. Sixteen inches fell in the Hayward area, and there were many reports of older structures collapsing under the heavy weight of the snow. The event became known as "The Halloween Storm of 1991." We were excited to see the early snowfall, as it assured good hunting conditions for the entire deer season.

We arrived at camp on Friday, November 22, to find the forest floor covered in wet snow. The woods were full of water, as it had rained for several days following the Halloween Storm event. On the first Saturday of season, we awoke to several inches of new snow. It was rough going in the woods, but we managed to get three deer on the opening weekend. Dennis shot a small buck on the following Tuesday, and the next day we received an additional six inches of snow. I found myself struggling to walk through the heavy snow in the woods, troubled by a hernia I had gotten by lifting up and draining a boat filled with rainwater. I was delaying having surgery for the hernia repair until after deer season. Several of us remained in camp for Thanksgiving Day and were joined by our other family members for a celebration. The following day was Friday and the start of the last weekend of deer season. We had numerous either-sex permits that year, and Ollie shot three deer from his tree stand just as it began to snow very heavily about 3:30. By 5 o'clock that day, it was obvious we were in for some very nasty winter weather. As the evening progressed, Dennis was increasingly concerned about our safety and getting snowed in. He was very worried about the older Jolly Boys. What if they developed a medical condition? How would we get them out? Would the snow load collapse the roof of our thirty-five-year-old hunting shack? How would we get the Coot back out to the road? How would we be able to transport the seven deer hanging on the buck pole along with all of the gear everyone had? How would I be able to make it back out to the road with my hernia condition, walking in waist-deep snow? Dennis was a mess and on the verge of hyperventilating. About 2 a.m. on Saturday, Dennis left his bunk and woke up my son Rob to assist him in firing up the Coot. The two of them were going to try to bust a trail to the highway and keep the road open. About twelve inches of snow had already fallen, and the Coot didn't operate well in the snow. Although the two of them made several trips back and forth between the shack and the highway where our cars were parked, they finally abandoned their efforts just as dawn was breaking. There was simply too much snow. Seventeen inches of new snow had fallen overnight to add to what was already on the ground.

Everyone was up early that morning and we developed an escape plan while having our morning coffee. Rob and Ollie would walk out to the highway and dig out a vehicle. They would then go to town to get Ollie's snowmobile for transportation and my dad's snow-blower to blow out a path to get our vehicles dug out. The rest of us would stay at camp and cut up the seven deer we had harvested that deer season. We would then play poker until they returned to rescue us.

We spent the day skinning out and cutting up the seven deer, and by mid-afternoon Rob and Ollie came ramming through the woods on Ollie's snowmobile. There was jubilation—we had been "rescued"! They brought good news. Adder had been unable to join us for the final weekend of deer camp and knew we were snow-bound and in trouble. He had sent my cousin up with his pickup and plow to clear a path through the snow so we could drive out onto the highway. We were feeling some relief. The cards were dealt, and we all enjoyed a final Saturday evening in the hunting camp surrounded by a winter wonderland.

On Sunday morning, the trek from the shack to the main highway began, and it was quite a project. Ollie had driven his snowmobile back and forth between the shack and the highway numerous times to bust a trail open and pack the snow down but we still had to get the Coot out to the highway. We loaded it with our gear and the venison. We then hooked the snowmobile to the front of the Coot, and everyone assisted in shoving the Coot and the snowmobile down the trail as the snowmobile struggled and smoked, trying to pull the Coot to the highway. After a morning of hard work, we were successful, and everyone was able to get his vehicle out onto the highway except for Bobby's old beat-up Buick, which was still

stuck in the snow. He lovingly referred to that old wreck as his "deer hunting car." I attached a tow strap to his rear bumper, and we tried to pull it free with a four-wheel drive Jeep, but the bumper of that old rusty Buick ripped off and went flying through the snow. Bobby was upset over the damage to his deer hunting car but took it in stride. We shoveled his vehicle out by hand and loaded his bumper into his back seat. He left all of us standing there chuckling as he left for Superior.

A few weeks later I had my planned hernia surgery. While I was recovering at home, I became inspired to write a poem to send to everyone to record the event of getting snowed in:

'Twas the last Friday, season's end was drawing near;
    Snowflakes started falling, we were running low on beer.
Ollie had just killed three, the time was almost four;
    Getting dark and nasty, snow on forest floor.
Seven deer had been taken, one was quite small;
    No problem there, twas better than none at all.
Dennis looked worried, concerned about the weather;
    Pacing back and forth, working up such a tether.
"John's got a hernia! Marvin's getting old,
    How the heck we getting back out to the road?"
"The Coot won't make it, the snow's really thick!
    Anyone in the outhouse? I think I have to ****!"
John said, "Chill out, Dennis, we've got plenty to eat,
    Somehow we'll make it, let's take care of the meat.

Haul 'em in the shack, hang them by upper bunk;
Stoke up the fires, we'll drink and get drunk.
Forget about the weather, we'll cut them up at dawn;
All the big deer, and Russ' buck fawn."
The cards were dealt, but Dennis really got nervous;
He threw on his boots, "Let's put the Coot into service"!
Snow kept on falling, as the Coot left the shack;
Dennis at the wheel, and Rob shovin' in the back.
One hour later, two snowmen did appear;
Dennis totally white, and Rob still pushing in the rear.
All through the night, Dennis laid in his bed;
With visions of tragedy dancing through his head.
Up every two hours, to bust a trail to the road;
Almost a useless effort, wasted in the cold.
Dawn finally came, seventeen inches had fallen;
The commo phone bell dinged twice, who could be callin'?
It was Peter with Adder, wondering of our plight;
Were we stranded and okay? Had we made it through the night?
Adder wanted to come in, but there was no place to park;
We told him to forget it, he couldn't disembark.
Rob and Ollie left for town, marching waist deep in snow;
Rob's Jeep wouldn't start, and he had to locate a tow.
The boys were on a mission, Ollie's snowmobile we would need;
The Coot no longer would make it, to this we would concede.
Several hours later, came a-crashing down the trail;
Two smiling Hanson kids, their mission did not fail.
We had been rescued, the meat was finally cut;

On with the game, forget about the "rut"!
The phone dinged again, 'twas Craig Hanson on the line;
Adder had sent him, and he plowed us out in time.
The crisis almost over, Dennis began to feel great;
Took paper sack off his head, no longer would he
hyperventilate.
The hunters were at peace now, and enjoyed their Saturday night;
Sunday would be a breeze, after experiencing such a fright.
The exodus went smoothly, as we trailered out our gear;
Sunday at ten, we finally ran out of beer.
The last task before us was to pull out the Coot;
Dennis said, "Leave it till summer, I really don't give a hoot."
We tied Ollie's snowmobile with a strap to the Coot's front;
Several started pushing, did they ever groan and grunt.
It was quite an ordeal, but somehow we got out;
It wasn't very easy, but accomplished with muscle and clout.
The last task at hand, pull Bobby's car from the snow;
Just hook up the tow strap, and away he would go.
The tow strap was connected, between the two cars;
It was stretched and tied, between rear face-bars.
Russ' Jeep pulled and tightened, the long nylon strap;
The next thing we heard, was a soft breaking crack.
There laid Bobby's bumper, away it did go;
Flying from his Buick, and sliding through the snow.
All we could hear, was a voice from afar;
What the **** have you guys done, to my deer hunting car?!?!

Soon after the deer season of 1991, Ollie showed up sporting a new customized license plate on the back of his four-wheel-drive pickup truck: "SNOWDIN".

Butchering the Deer

Butchering a deer is very much like the art of properly field-dressing a deer. It's not something that one does every day. The first time one is called upon to do it, it is a very foreign technique. The second time is easier, as one knows what to expect. Like everything else, the more times one is exposed to dressing out a deer or cutting it up, the more proficient one becomes, and eventually it becomes second nature.

In the early years at Blue Heaven, cutting up the venison was not a major problem, as there weren't many deer in the area, and not many deer were taken during the deer season. More often than not, there were only one or two deer that were shot by the Jolly Boys over the course of the entire season, and those deer were skinned and cut up to eat while the hunters were still up at deer camp. In the years that followed, when deer became more plentiful and more than one or two deer were harvested, plans had to be made to butcher the animals after deer season.

My father was a very skilled butcher. Everyone who watched him cut up meat thought he had the skills of an experienced surgeon. He had been in the grocery business the majority of his life and had spent a considerable amount of time behind the meat counter. There was little he didn't know about meat and how to cut it up properly. He had the various butchering tools to prove it, with a vast collection of Chicago Cutlery that he had accumulated over the years. All of his knives were kept in a special cloth carrying-case and all were always razor-sharp. Fellow Jolly Boy Merle and Russ Clagett were also well versed on how to cut up a deer, having learned the skill from others during their many years of deer hunting.

It was a tedious chore to cut up the deer once deer season had ended. They were taken to my father's garage and hung from the rafters. The hunters selected a day to meet at my parent's house to tackle the chore, usually in very cold weather, and usually the deer were completely frozen. The hunters would go to the garage with their knives and "skin" the frozen hides off the deer, cutting the deer into sections to be brought into the house for further processing. By the time this task was completed, everyone had stiff hands from working in the cold. We all chipped in to accomplish the various tasks, and each person had a job to do dependent on his individual skill level. Some would be involved in "boning out" the meat, which is removing the meat from the bones. Others would use knives to remove the tallow from the meat make sure that the meat was as free of hair and tallow as possible. Lots of damp paper towels were used in the process of removing stray deer hair, and the meat was sorted into piles for steaks, stew meat, hamburger, and roasts. The project would usually start mid-afternoon on the selected day, and it would be late in the evening before everything had been cut up, wrapped, and labeled. The meat would then be equally divided by the hunters except for the coveted sirloins and tenderloins, which were reserved for special Jolly Boy events. My mother's kitchen ended up in a complete mess during this process, but she never complained.

As the years passed and deer became more plentiful, cutting up the meat after deer season became too much of a chore to accomplish in my parents' kitchen, so the Jolly Boys came to the decision that it made sense to butcher the deer up at the deer camp during the final weekend of the deer season. The deer we had harvested were taken to town, registered with the DNR, and then brought back to camp for butchering. With all of the skill and manpower we had at hand, no one ever gave a thought to taking the deer to a butcher shop for processing, nor did the Jolly Boys ever consider turning the venison into sausage, brats, or beer sticks. They enjoyed the natural flavor of venison too much. On the last Friday of the season, the deer were brought inside the shack and hung from the rafters so they would thaw overnight. A plastic tarp was laid on the floor to catch any loose hair or blood from the thawing animals. After an early breakfast the next morning, we would begin removing the deer hides in the warmth of the hunting shack so they could be butchered. I'm certain my mother was overjoyed that we had relieved her of the burden of cleaning up the mess in her kitchen after these sessions. Moreover, butchering the deer while at deer camp was the perfect way to pass deer-butchering skills from father to son.

Once the deer hides were removed, the deer carcasses were ready to be cut into sections and taken outside to be kept cool. We always hung the deer by their hind legs to facilitate the skinning and butchering. Once they were skinned, a meat saw was used to remove the head, along with the attached deer hide. Then the neck would be cut off to be turned into a neck roast or boned out for stew or hamburger meat. The front shoulders were cut off next to be saved for roasts or boned out for stew or hamburger meat. It then took three men to cut off the main body of the deer from the hind quarters. Two men had to hold the heavy main body while a third man cut and sawed until it detached from the hindquarters. Finally, the two hindquarters were each cut into two sections.

Once the deer were all skinned and sectioned, we cleaned up any mess that we'd made and prepared for the process of cutting up and wrapping all of the venison. The large lumberjack table on which we dined served as our butcher block, with a multitude of cutting boards lying on the table. Almost everyone at our camp had his own favorite set of knives that he used for boning out and cutting up the meat. We started by bringing in the main body section of the deer which contains the ribs and sirloins. The sirloins, which many refer to as "back-straps," run along the top back spine of the deer. The tenderloins run along the underside of the spine. Usually, the tenderloins had already been removed by us right after the deer was killed. This is because they were easily accessible once the deer had been field- dressed, and if they weren't removed right away, they would dry out and this coveted piece of meat wouldn't be much good. Any salvageable meat left on the main section was cut away and put in a pile to be ground into hamburger, which is excellent in both chili and spaghetti recipes. The Jolly Boys never did anything with the venison ribs, as they contained too much strong tallow; these usually were discarded and put out for the chickadees to enjoy. The loins were wrapped whole in freezer paper and cut into steaks at a future time, just before being flash-fried at a special event. The front shoulders would then be brought in, cleaned up, and cut into roasts. A considerable amount of time was spent cleaning up the hindquarters and as much round steak would be cut from them as possible. Any scraps would be thrown in a bucket for stew meat or grinding into hamburger. Depending on how many deer had to be butchered, it was usually a process that took the entire morning and afternoon before everything was wrapped in freezer paper and labeled. Nothing went to waste. The venison was just too coveted for that to happen. Even the deer hides were taken to town and sold to be made into gloves and clothing. When the Jolly Boys finished butchering a deer, the only thing left was the deer hoofs, and even those were often given away to someone who had a use for them.

Frozen deer hanging from the open rafters of the shack on the last weekend of deer season near the heat of the wood stove. Once thawed, the hides can be easily removed and the deer cut into sections for butchering.

Russ Clagett using his favorite boning knife to carefully remove the sirloins from the upper portion of the spine. Scrap meat will be boned out for hamburger.

(L-R) Dennis Clagett getting instruction from his father Russ Clagett on how to boneout a hind quarter while Brian Hanson removes excess fat and deer hairs from the venison prior to cutting and wrapping it for the freezer.

Russ Clagett uses a meat saw to make a rump roast from a hind quarter while Marv Hanson works at boning out and cutting up steaks to be wrapped.

1992-1993

The winter of 1992 was a banner year for snow. The shack log has multiple entries of many of us who snowmobiled or cross-country-skied in to Blue Heaven to keep the roof shoveled and have a weekend party or two. The following fall, it was once again time to level the shack in addition to cutting wood for the upcoming deer season. The shack had been built on wood and concrete block piers without any footings, and each spring it would become unleveled because of the heavy clay soil which caused several of the piers to either sink or rise with the spring thaw. It was a constant battle but a chore that had to be undertaken or else the doors and windows wouldn't function properly. We would have to crawl under the shack, which sat only about a foot off the ground, with hydraulic jacks and raise or lower certain areas in our attempt to level it. My mother often quipped that we had the only self-cleaning table she had ever seen, because if someone accidentally spilled a drink on it, the liquid would quickly run off because the table was not even close to being level.

There were eight of us in attendance for that deer season. Although the deer in Wisconsin were reported as being plentiful, there was very little deer sign in the area where we hunt. The only deer we shot was a six-point buck, even though we possessed several hunter's-choice and bonus-deer permits. Ollie finally got impatient and went north to hunt with some friends in the Eau Claire Lakes area, bringing us back a doe for camp meat. After the season ended, the reports were that the deer harvest in our area was down fifty percent from the previous year. Merle didn't attend deer camp with us that year. He was beginning to spend less and less time up at the shack during deer season, choosing instead to go to another deer camp north of us with Adder's oldest son, Peter. Peter loved to hunt but had multiple allergies. One of those allergies was smoke from cigars and cigarettes, and the other allergy was deer hair. Adder's youngest son, Phillip, had married a woman who also liked to hunt, so Phillip opted to hunt with her and her family in the Phillips area. We knew Merle still loved Blue Heaven, but he frequently felt more relaxed hunting at a camp where there were only two or three other hunters and things were more peaceful.

The following year provided no either-sex permits for hunters in our area during the deer season. Due to the low deer herd, it had returned to a buck-only season, and we all speculated that the heavy snows of the winter of 1991-1992 had taken their toll on the deer and fawn crop. We had very little snow on the ground for the 1993 season until Thanksgiving Day, when we finally received five inches of new snow. We hunted hard for the last weekend of the hunt, but no deer were seen, and there were very few deer tracks observed. It was a disappointing season because we didn't get any venison for our table, but we all still thoroughly enjoyed deer camp. Adder was really beginning to show his 83 years that season. He no longer had any desire to leave the shack to hunt but would instead stay behind doing a few odd kitchen chores, sitting at the table reading, or taking frequent naps. He had developed a sleep problem. He was unable to sleep at night and would end up being in his bunk for most of the daylight hours and pacing around in the shack in the dead of night when the rest of us were in our bunks. We finally took him into town to see his doctor to determine if something could be done to correct his sleep patterns.

Changing of the Guard

During deer season 1993, several things were put into motion that would change things at the hunting shack for many years to come. The hunting camp was now almost 40 years old and only three of the original Jolly Boys remained: my father, Adder, and Merle. It became obvious to Dennis and me that it was becoming increasingly difficult for the three of them to handle all of the responsibilities of ownership of the shack. Adder was in his 80s and had developed sleeping issues, my father was in his mid-seventies, and Merle wasn't far behind, showing less and less interest in coming to Blue Heaven for deer season. Dennis and I were becoming concerned about the future of the hunting camp and wanted to take action to preserve the tradition. Although my father was still very active in our camp, he was less able to gather all of the supplies and handle cooking chores. None of the original Jolly Boys were able to perform much maintenance of the shack, due to their age.

Dennis and his father had been regular members of the hunting camp for almost twenty-five years, and we all considered them honorary Jolly Boys. Dennis and I decided that we would attempt to purchase the hunting camp from the Jolly Boys to assure that the two of us, his father, and my two sons would always have this hunting camp to go to every fall.

Towards the end of the deer season, I approached my father with the thought that Dennis and I would purchase the camp. My father was well aware that the original Jolly Boys agreement spelled out that no one Jolly Boy could sell his share in the camp, as the agreement was that if a Jolly Boy left or died, his share would pass to the survivors. He was also aware that I was trying to come up with a solution to enable things to remain the same as each of the three remaining Jolly Boys passed away or could no longer be there to hunt. He also felt strongly that someday the camp should be in the hands of his grandsons, as they were the logical ones to someday have ownership.

We all knew that the hunting shack wasn't worth much money. The building was showing a great deal of wear and tear, and the contents within had outlived their useful life quite some time ago. The hunting camp was situated on land leased to the Jolly Boys by the county; therefore, only real property would be involved in the sale. There was no real estate, but Dennis and I were fine with that. We knew that we'd only be purchasing tradition and a lot of memories and making certain that Blue Heaven would continue to thrive once the original Jolly Boys were no longer around. I knew that in order to convince Adder and Merle to sell, they would need to have assurances that they wouldn't be excluded for so long as they both were alive and wanted to come to the shack. I therefore drafted a purchase agreement to present to them and my father.

The purpose of the agreement was to supersede any previous agreements that had been made by the five original Jolly Boys regarding the hunting camp. The agreement spelled out that although ownership of the camp and the responsibilities of operating the camp would be transferred to Dennis and me, the Jolly Boys would be granted all of the privileges that they had previously enjoyed and would retain the rights to their assigned bunks and lockers for so long as they desired to participate in the hunting camp. We also assured the Jolly Boys that all of the established rules would continue unchanged to assure that the camp continued to perpetuate itself.

It wasn't difficult to convince the Jolly Boys to sell the camp at this point, as they all felt that the burden of maintaining the camp needed to be passed on and it was time for someone else to manage the finances and take care of the insurance, taxes, and camp permit. We easily agreed on a purchase price, and in January of 1994, Dennis and I became the owners of Blue Heaven, and the recreational use permit was transferred into our names. It was a win-win situation for everyone, and Dennis and I believed that we were capable of continuing the tradition of the Jolly Boys and Blue Heaven for years to come.

1994–V&MM

We had a devastating discovery at the shack when we arrived for the annual spring frolic and work party on Friday, April 15, 1994. Sometime after deer season 1993, someone had broken into the shack and had made a mess of the place.

The weather that weekend was horrible. The temperature was in the lower 40s with a strong wind, abundant rain, and heavy snow showers. The road in to the shack was full of water. Ollie had buried his new pickup in a mud hole, attempting to drive in with the supplies. We arrived on foot, cold and wet, to find that the glass out of the two doors had been broken to gain entry, and the vandals had also broken one of the large windows. Glass was everywhere, but nothing appeared to be missing. We spent the rest of the evening hauling in our supplies by hand and attempting to secure the shack for the night by putting plastic over the broken doors and window. We weren't able to eat our supper until 11 p.m. that evening, and it took until midnight to finally get the shack warmed up to where it was comfortable enough to retire for the evening.

The next day dawned clear and mild, but it was still very windy. We spent the morning digging the pickup out of the mud and then made a trip into town to pick up replacement glass to repair the doors and windows. Several stayed at camp to finish cleaning up all of the debris from the damage and to wash all of the dishes and everything else that had been exposed to the elements for several months. By Saturday night, things had pretty much returned to normal, and we left the shack on Sunday afternoon with thoughts of concern over possible future break-ins and vandalism. Several inspection trips were made into the shack over the course of that summer. To our relief, there was no further vandalism discovered.

The potential for burglary and vandalism to our hunting shack has always been of major concern. The place sits unoccupied for months at a time, and it is deep in the woods, far off the beaten path. It's a risk that we've had to accept. We consider ourselves fortunate that, for the most part, people who pass by our camp respect the fact that it is property belonging to others, and their curiosity to see what's inside vanishes as they pass by.

In August 1994, my dad—the best of the Jolly Boys, in my opinion—died. His heart stopped suddenly. Although they helicoptered him to Eau Claire, where valiant efforts were made to revive him, his doctors informed us that there was nothing that could be done, and we ultimately made the decision to have all of his life-support systems removed. His passing had a profound and lasting impact on Blue Heaven. His skill at organizing the trips in to the shack would be greatly missed and difficult to replace, and we all knew there would be a massive void at deer season and the other events held at Blue Heaven.

Marvin and Violet proving that happiness is a perfectly cooked prime rib roast from the wood-stove oven for their friends and guests at Blue Heaven.

Prime Rib of Beef Roast

Whenever the Jolly Boys desired the ultimate festive evening meal at our hunting camp, they looked to prime rib to fill that need. Properly prepared and served with *au jus* and horseradish sauce, along with side dishes of garlic mashed potatoes and a great salad or asparagus wrapped in bacon, prime rib makes one feel as if they are dining at an exclusive supper club. Prime rib is nothing more than un-cut rib eye steak which is still in the form of a roast, and rib eyes are said to be one of the most popular cuts of steak.

My father taught me three things about purchasing and preparing prime rib properly. The first thing I needed to learn was that when you go to the grocery store or meat market and ask to purchase a prime rib roast, you're probably not actually purchasing "prime" rib. Beef is graded according to the marbling in the meat. The marbling is the small white swirls of fat, which make the beef tender and flavorful. Prime is the best grade and also the most expensive. More often than not, it needs to be special ordered from your butcher in advance. They don't sell many prime cuts because of the price, so they rarely have a prime rib roast in their meat case.

The majority of prime beef cuts are sold to only the most exclusive restaurants by the distributor. Most often, your butcher will have a "choice" prime rib roast on hand, and although it is a grade down from prime, it still has excellent marbling and is about half the cost of prime. After prime and choice are the "select" cuts of beef. Forget about "select." It has very little marbling and is very lean. You can't purchase a bad cut of meat and make it better by cooking it. As the saying goes, you get what you pay for.

He then taught me about purchasing the correct "cut." The preferred cut is a "standing rib roast." from which the bones have not been removed. When you cook it, the ribs should be placed in the roasting pan bone-side-down, with the fat side of the prime rib up so the fat juices of the meat penetrate the roast as it is cooking. The standing rib roast is usually available only around the major holiday seasons of Thanksgiving, Christmas, and New Year's Eve. During other times of the year, the roast is usually sold bone-out, but both are equally good. If you are fortunate and find a standing rib roast, figure that each rib will feed about two people. If you purchase a bone-out roast, figure about one-half to three quarters of a pound of meat per person. There's considerable waste on a great prime rib roast.

Finally, I learned from my father how to prepare and cook the roast, a skill at which he had a great deal of expertise. Use a sharp knife and score the top fat section of the roast in a diamond pattern, cutting into the fat about one quarter-inch deep. Use a liberal amount of fresh minced garlic or prepared garlic from the jar and rub the garlic down into the slits of the fat for flavoring. Also coat the top fat layer with a liberal amount of rock salt and coarsely ground pepper. Place the roast in a shallow roasting pan, one that has edges about one-to-two inches high to catch the juices of the roast as it cooks. The juices will be used later to make *au jus* to serve with the roast. Place the uncovered roast in a very hot pre-heated oven and cook it for about 15 minutes at around 450 degrees. The extreme heat will sear the roast to lock in all of the natural moisture. Reduce the oven temperature to 325 degrees and allow about 15 minutes per pound to produce a medium-rare roast. Always use a meat thermometer to track the internal temperature of the roast. As a guide, when the center of the roast is 115-120 degrees, it is rare; at 130-135 degrees, it is medium-rare; and 140-145 degrees it is medium. Keep in mind that when you remove the roast from the oven, it will still cook for a bit, so allow for a 5- to 10-degree temperature rise once the roast is out of the oven and "resting" prior to being cut and served.

We find that most people prefer their prime rib either medium-rare or on the rare side. The center of a medium-rare roast is on the rare side, while the end cuts are medium, and the rest of the roast should be medium-rare when the internal temperature reaches 130 degrees.

The three most important factors in preparing the perfect prime rib roast are allowing the roast to "rest" before cutting and serving it, removing the roast from the oven before it becomes over-cooked, and never piercing the roast with forks.

When your roast has reached its desired internal temperature, remove it from the roasting pan and place it on your serving platter with an aluminum "tent" on top of the roast. Allow the roast to rest for about 30 minutes. If you cut and serve the roast immediately after removing it from the oven, the hot juices within the roast will bleed out and be extracted from the meat, and you will lose much of its flavor and tenderness. Always allow the roast to rest.

If your roast becomes over-cooked, you can't fix it. It's better to remove the roast from the oven earlier rather than later because if the roast is slightly undercooked, it can be fixed with an easy trick. If some of your guests find that their serving is too rare for them, simply take their slice of prime rib using tongs and place it in simmering *au jus* for 10-15 seconds. A rare piece of prime rib will magically become medium-rare in a few seconds, and a medium-rare piece can be transformed into medium in the same time frame. It's always better to under-cook rather than over-cook the roast.

Never use sharp serving forks to stab and place the roast in the baking pan or to remove the roast from the oven. You want to lock in all of the natural juices. Any penetration of the roast during the cooking process will allow the natural juices to flow from the roast through those holes while it is cooking.

AU JUS AND HORSERADISH SAUCE

While the roast is "resting," place the roasting pan with the roast juices on the stovetop and use moderate heat to bring it to a simmer, scraping the bottom of the pan to blend everything together. Add about three cups of water and a tablespoon of beef bouillon paste along with two tablespoons of prepared horseradish. Once this mixture is simmering, add either a cup of red wine or a cup of brandy to kick things up a notch. Serve the *au jus* in small individual bowls and use the remaining *au jus* to quickly dip any prime rib that requires additional cooking.

Horseradish sauce is an elegant accessory to go with the prime rib and is prepared by using two cups of sour cream and one-quarter to one-half cup of horseradish. Blend together and place in a serving dish and put it on the table.

One of our favorite meals in deer camp during the hunting season is a huge medium-rare prime rib roast that has been cooked to perfection on high heat in the old wood burning stove. It is usually served with horseradish sauce and au jus laced with brandy, shack-baked potatoes with ample butter and sour cream, and a Caesar salad. In this photo, Ollie is shown doing the honors of carving while his older brother Rob patiently waits for the others to be served.

Deer Season 1994

When deer season 1994 arrived, all of us knew that things at Blue Heaven would be different than in past years. My dad was no longer a part of the group, and that had left a huge void. Due to his advanced age, Adder declined to join us for the hunt. Merle also advised us that he wouldn't be in attendance opening weekend, as he was fighting a virus and wasn't feeling well. For the first time, there were no Jolly Boys in camp on opening day.

Seven of us were there for opening weekend. I, along with my new partner Dennis, Dennis' dad Russ, my son Ollie, and my dad's brother Bobby were there, as were Bobby's son Brian and a good friend of mine from Colfax, Barry Rice. Both Brian and Barry had hunted with us previously. They had now become a part of our permanent group and were always in regular attendance. Robin was out of the state, working at a new job, and couldn't make it for the season. While Ollie was in transit from school in Michigan to the shack, he hit a deer with his truck, providing us with camp meat at the beginning of the season.

Deer season that year came and went without much fanfare. There were the usual card games and great food, and although we managed to shoot a couple of deer during the hunt, there would be no tales of monster bucks being shot. Merle was finally able to come up for one night, and it was great to finally have a Jolly Boy back in camp with us. Over the course of the season, there were more than just a few tears shed remembering my father. He had been a mentor to both of my sons, and they were having a very difficult time coming to grips with the fact that he would no longer be occupying his chair at the head of the table.

Towards the end of the season, Adder sent word that he wanted us to pack up any belongings that he had at Blue Heaven and bring them back into town with us when we broke camp for the season. Although Adder would still make a trip or two to the shack over the years for an evening visit with dinner, he would never again be occupying his bunk at Blue Heaven. His nights were too broken with insomnia.

Deer Season 1995

In the early summer of 1995, the Sawyer County Conservation and Forestry Committee made a recommendation that the recreational use permits for the 100 cabins on county forest lands be included in the next ten-year forest-management plan. We were all relieved that the lease for Blue Heaven would be safe for at least the next ten years. It seemed like the only party opposed to the permits was the Wisconsin Department of Natural Resources. I, like my father before me, penned a letter to the local newspaper praising the Forestry Committee for their decision to continue the permits and voicing my disapproval over the DNR's lack of cooperation and foresight to continue the camps.

The transition of the group coming to Blue Heaven continued in 1995 with the addition of Ollie's close friend, Brian Lane. We now had both Brian Hanson who had been hunting with us for several years and Brian Lane coming to the shack. In order to keep the confusion of similar names to a minimum, we nicknamed Brian Hanson "Billie-Bob" because he was an avid NASCAR fan, and gave Brian Lane the nickname "City-Billy" because he hailed from the

Twin Cities area. Although we all missed the Jolly Boys of yesteryear, Dennis and I were both thrilled to see the influx of younger hunters joining our group. We strongly felt that having younger men hunting with us would greatly increase our chances of getting more deer during deer season, and their ability to assist with all of the camp chores would be most welcome.

Billie-Bob was the son of my father's brother Bobby. He had lost some favor with my father back in the mid-1970s on his first visit to the shack, when he was in his early 20s. He had a wee bit too much to drink one evening and fell asleep at the table after everyone else had retired for the evening. Normally, someone falling asleep at the table wouldn't have been a problem, but he had loaded the wood stove with wood with the stove drafts wide open. My father awoke from deep slumber smelling the shack filling with smoke and hearing the fire roaring. He leaped from his bunk and rushed to the stove to turn the drafts off and secure the stove lid. In my father's eyes, this event was a cardinal sin, and my Uncle Bobby was calmly informed by my father that Brian would no longer be welcome at Blue Heaven. It took quite a number of years before my father finally felt that Brian was mature enough to come up to Blue Heaven again. It was a lesson learned and remembered. Brian quickly earned his way back into my father's good graces and became a valued member of the hunting shack.

All bunks were filled for the opening deer hunting weekend that year, but no Jolly Boys were there. There was more deer sign and deer seen in our area than what had been seen in over a decade. After three days of hunting, we had five deer hanging from the deer pole, and the season proved to be a banner year for Wisconsin deer hunters. There were 684,944 licensed hunters in the woods that season and they bagged a total of 398,002 deer, equating to a success ratio of about 58%. We had nine hunters in our camp bagging five deer, for a success ratio of 56%. Needless to say, we were pleased with our results and the management of the deer herd.

Merle and Adder came up for an evening of card-playing and a great dinner of venison on the first Monday night of that season, but neither of them showed any interest in staying overnight at Blue Heaven. When they walked into the bunk area to examine their old bunks, we could see that they were remembering days past at Blue Heaven. It was as if we were treating them as guests in their own home, and we all felt strange as we watched them walk out the door and leave for town that evening. We had had eleven around our table for dinner that night. For a moment, it seemed like the dinner parties of old that the Jolly Boys used to have up at camp, but we never even came close to duplicating the antics that they used to have at Blue Heaven.

GHOSTS

In late October of 1996, Ollie and his friend City-Billie, along with their friend Derrick, decided to go up to the shack on the night before the rest of us arrived for the annual fall work party so they could open up the camp and get the fires going. It was a cold and windy October evening, and the three of them had arrived too late to think about preparing a dinner for themselves. They settled for drinks and multiple snacks while they enjoyed playing cards.

When the rest of us arrived the next morning, they related a story of an encounter that they all swore they had had around midnight. The three of them had enjoyed ample drinks and had grown tired of playing cards, and they were talking about turning in for the night. There was a huge gust of wind. The three of them simultaneously looked over at the window above the kitchen sink, where all three saw what appeared to be a face peering through the window at them. Thinking that it might be one of us arriving late that evening, they all went outside to greet the new arrival but found no one there. They walked around the outside of the shack but saw neither man nor beast lurking in the shadows. Naturally, the three of them were somewhat shaken by this strange encounter. Ollie even speculated that it might be the spirit of his grandfather peeking in at them as they enjoyed their evening at Blue Heaven. The shack log records their encounter in a poem.

"Twas the week before Halloween, and all around the shack
Ghosts and goblins haunted the door in the back.
Ollie, Brian, and Derrick had arrived the night before,
And swore there were ghosts peeking through the door.
Could it be real spooks, or brains that were numb
From late hours of drinking too much whiskey and rum?"

THE SPOOK

After Merle, Dennis, Russ, Bobby, Billie-Bob, Barry, and I got settled in with our gear for the weekend, we all got busy completing various tasks around camp in preparation for the 1996 deer season. Once again we needed to re-level the shack; cut, split, and stack the wood; change the oil in the light plant, and perform numerous minor repairs.

We were just about ready to take a break and have our Saturday noon lunch, when appearing out of nowhere was an unclean-looking individual riding his bike up the logging trail leading to our shack. We were all confused as to why someone would be riding a bike this deep in the woods. He was wearing a backpack and appeared to be homeless. He stopped, got off his bike, rolled and lit up a joint, and asked us all if we wanted "a hit." We all politely declined his offer and asked him what he was doing so deep in the woods. He responded that he was "looking for jack pines." All of us knew that there weren't any jack pines within 20 miles. However, we pointed to the road and told him he would have to go back to the main highway and head north to find the trees he was looking for. He reeked of pot and we all knew he was a total dope head and we were all anxious for him to leave the area. He finally did leave. There was then considerable speculation as to whether he had been the "spook" appearing at the window the evening before. We were also concerned that he might have been eyeing up Blue Heaven as a place in which to live after we left for the weekend. Fortunately, we never saw him again.

Church Barbeques

I've always been amazed at how many groceries the younger guys at our camp can go through when they sit down at the table. Their hunger appears to be impossible to satisfy when everyone is up there working so hard, and it's always a challenge to make certain ample food is placed on the table for their consumption. In years past, we usually served fried hamburgers for lunch when we were at the shack in the spring and fall for work parties. Some of these guys could easily polish off three hamburgers. I therefore looked for a menu item that would satisfy them, yet keep costs within our limited budget. The answer came in my mother's "church barbeque" recipe. I don't know who should receive the credit for this recipe. All I can recall is my mother telling me that the recipe was developed by the ladies of her church to help stretch the hamburger when they were making barbeques for a church function. It is simple to prepare, and the flavor is excellent. This recipe will, hopefully, serve 8 to 10 people.

CHURCH BARBEQUES

Fry four pounds of 80/20 hamburger in a large skillet with one large, diced yellow onion. Liberally salt and pepper while it's frying. Once hamburger is cooked and broken into small pieces, drain excess grease from skillet. Add two 10.5-ounce cans of Campbell's chicken gumbo soup. Do not dilute soup with water. Add about one cup of catsup and about one-quarter cup of yellow mustard. Stir and cover, allowing ingredients to simmer for about an hour.

Serve on hamburger buns on paper plates with a fork. I usually will just put the pot on the table and allow people to serve themselves, as some like to eat the barbeques "open-faced." A handful of potato chips and a good kosher dill pickle go great with the barbeques.

I will also often make an easy chip-dip to go with the potato chips. This can be accomplished by taking a small container of sour cream and adding a teaspoon of garlic salt, along with few good shakes of dill weed.

Our War on Mice

Throughout the years, our hunting camp has been damaged by wind storms, hail storms, vandalism, theft, porcupines, and other perils that have harmed our beloved Blue Heaven. Some of the most frustrating damage has been caused by Mr. Mouse. Because the shack is in the middle of the woods and is unoccupied for the majority of time, the advantage goes to these destructive little creatures that seem to take up occupancy as soon as we lock the door.

The mice that we deal with are called "deer mice," or, in scientific terms, Peromyscus. They have big eyes and little ears that look like deer ears and are very agile compared to the common house mouse. They are extremely industrious. These mice have light brown fur and a white underbelly, and I find them to be somewhat cute.

Mr. Mouse started to appear in our hunting shack shortly after it was built. I recall being up there one weekend when my mother pulled open the silverware drawer, only to find mama mouse and her litter occupying the drawer in a nest built out of paper toweling. After the screaming stopped, my father grabbed the drawer and threw the contents out in the leaves. The silverware was triple-washed by my mother, and then washed again. After all, these little guys are noted for being carriers of multiple diseases. A year or two later, she was again surprised and found another nest in our linen drawer. More screaming, more throwing of contents into the woods. My mother was a farm girl, familiar with all sorts of critters, but she didn't think that mice were "cute." When I was young, I always slept in the center upper bunk directly below an old moldy mounted deer head. One evening, as I crawled into my sleeping bag, I thought I had a vision that the old deer head was actually moving. Closer examination revealed that Mrs. Mouse and her large family had built a nest in the forehead of that old mount, which was teeming with activity. No screaming, but my father once again pitched valuable contents of the hunting shack out into the woods. The sad part is that the eight-point mount was the old buck head where we stuck our dollars on the deer horns for the hunter who shot the first buck. We now simply use an ice-pick to attach the dollar bills on the wall.

For years we tolerated the mice. After all, it was we who had invaded their territory, and we had to cohabitate with them or burn the shack down. I even recall one night when the little guys were racing around on the open rafters in the ceiling. We had great sport trying to nail one of them with an icepick, but they were much too fast and agile for us. Our quest to control them with various traps and poisons also proved unsuccessful.

One fall weekend Dennis Clagett went out to crank up the light plant, because it was getting dark, and mice came running out of the light plant as it began to start. The light plant was cooled by a fan and radiator attached to the engine, and mice had built a nest inside the fan. Dennis came into the shack to announce his personal war on our mouse issues. In the weeks and months that followed, he spent considerable time caulking, plugging holes with steel wool, nailing boards over cracks, setting traps, and putting out poison. This was war and he was going to win.

Dennis was successful in controlling the mice around the camp for quite a number of years. With the amount of d-CON that he put in the area, we all figured there wasn't a mouse within three miles. But ten years later the mice were back with a vengeance. The hunting shack was aging. Having been built on piers with only clay soil to support the place, the shack was settling, and new cracks and entry points provided opportunities for nesting and breeding. We had won the battle but not the war. More steel wool, more caulking, more d-CON, and more traps were put out.

My son Ollie decided it was time to intervene and came up with a solution for our mouse problems. He went on the Internet and found a new mouse trap aptly called "The Wheel of Death." It has been our salvation. The wheel is a simple contraption for eliminating mice. One takes an old bucket, pokes a hole on two sides, and runs a coat-hanger wire through the holes. Then, an empty tuna can with the lid still attached or an empty plastic pop bottle with the cap still on it has holes punched through it. The can or bottle is threaded and centered on the coat-hanger in the middle of the bucket. This is the wheel, and the rigid coat hanger wire serves as the axle. The wheel is then coated with peanut butter. The bucket is partially filled with six or more inches of old motor oil or antifreeze so the liquid doesn't freeze when the weather turns cold. Finally, a wooden stick is leaned up against the bucket to serve as a ramp for the mouse to climb up to the rim of the bucket. The mouse smells and sees the peanut butter and crawls out on the wire to the wheel. As soon as the mouse reaches the wheel, the wheel starts spinning and the mouse falls off the wheel into the motor oil or antifreeze, quickly drowning.

To add a little sport to the Wheel of Death, we started a pool to see who could guess how many mice would meet their demise over the course of the deer season. Everyone put in a dollar along with their guess. When we drained the pail at the end of the season, 37 mice were lying on the bottom. Unbelievable! Barry won the pool with his guess of 36.

The Wheel is probably not something that you would want sitting in the middle of your living room, but it works perfectly well for hunting shacks, garages, basements, and other areas where mice are abundant and need to be controlled.

KEMPS
FAMILY SIZE

1996-2000 Deer Seasons

As we entered the second half of the 1990s, it was obvious to all that our hunting camp continued to see major changes concerning the hunters who were now occupying the bunks at Blue Heaven. None of the original Jolly Boys were in attendance any longer. My father, Marvin, along with Kenny and Howard, had passed away, and Merle and Adder had lost much of their desire to join us during deer season. The patriarchs of our camp now consisted of my dad's brother Bobby and Dennis' father, Russ Clagett. Everyone else was much younger. The faces around the poker table were all familiar, but the absence of the original Jolly Boys was felt by everyone now hunting out of our hunting camp.

On a Tuesday evening during deer season 1997, Adder was able to return to the shack for one last meal of shack steak along with Merle. He was 87 years old. It was fantastic to see both Adder and Merle, the last of the Jolly Boys, sitting at their usual spots at the poker table that evening. Shortly before deer season, Merle's son, JK, had passed away of a stroke at the very young age of 47. John Kimball Dunster had been not only Merle's son but also my cousin and Dennis' brother-in-law. We all felt a huge void that he was no longer with us. He had been a big part of Blue Heaven in the earlier years before he left to join several other close friends of his who had established a new deer camp called "Camp Handicapped." One of the members, Tom, had lost his leg in the Vietnam War. Another member, Rolf, had lost his arm in a childhood accident. JK was a very kind person, with a remarkable sense of humor, and we had always enjoyed his companionship. We missed having him at Blue Heaven after he made the decision to begin hunting with his friends. JK frequently would relate a story about an evening when he and the other members of "Camp Handicapped" had paid a visit to a gentlemen's club named Phipps Tavern during deer season to partake in ogling some of the scantily dressed young ladies dancing there. One of these young ladies was dancing directly in front of their group, and they were trying to persuade her to come back to their hunting camp for a "private showing." After much debate, she finally lost her patience and told them, "Look, guys, it would take an arm and a leg for me to come back to your hunting shack with you." With that, Rolf took off his shirt, removed his artificial arm, and laid it on the bar, and Tom slid off his artificial leg from underneath his jeans and laid it on the bar. Most of the other hunters in the bar had been witnessing these negotiations, and the place broke out in riotous laughter when Tom and Rolf attempted to pay her price.

JK's memory would live on with all of us at Blue Heaven because shortly after JK passed away, Merle gave my younger son, Ollie, JK's old Jeep, which had been sitting in JK's garage deteriorating for several years. He had purchased the used 1966 Willy's CJ5 Jeep and had driven it for a number of years. When it began to be in a state of disrepair, he decided to park it in his garage, simply closing the garage door and leaving it there to rot. Merle gave the Jeep to Ollie in the summer of 1998. Ollie put the Jeep on a car trailer and hauled it home to begin the tedious project of rebuilding the vehicle. The tires were old and flat, the wheels and brakes were no good, there was rust throughout, and the engine needed to be overhauled. Ollie and his friend Brian Lane spent the summer rebuilding JK's old Jeep and drove it in to the hunting shack during deer season of that year. We were all amazed at the transformation of that old Jeep. Ollie and Brian had spent countless hours rebuilding it, and it was now a completely functional showpiece that we added to our arsenal of transportation used to maneuver the mud-holes in to the hunting camp.

Adder passed away in the comfort of his home in March of 1998 sitting fully dressed at his kitchen table, with his morning prune juice in front of him. He was such a big part of our hunting camp for over 40 years and was always overjoyed to be up there, even if it was only for an evening in the later years to enjoy a game of poker while sipping on a Manhattan. He would constantly reminisce about his many great memories of our hunting camp, as well as the hunting camps of old. He had left us with many stories about the history of Hayward and seemed to know everyone and how they fit into the history of the area. We all regretted that he had not taken the time to put all those stories on paper or cassette, even though we had encouraged him to do so. He had truly been a historian and had possessed knowledge that was unequaled. Our hunting camp sent a huge blue bouquet of flowers to his well-attended funeral, along with a poem that summed up our love of this man.

Thanks for the memories, for all those stories you shared;
Thanks for having been with us, we'll miss how much you cared.
Thanks for giving us those traditions we cherish at hunting camp;
We'll miss your wisdom and your company when we light the
Aladdin Lamp.
Thanks for everything that you left us to remember;
You will always be among us when we gather in November.

Shortly after Adder's passing, we learned that Russ Clagett had developed a serious medical condition called "Wegener's disease," which attacks a person's vital organs. Sadly, he succumbed to the disease shortly before his 81st birthday in August of 1998. Once again, we all found ourselves coping with the loss of one of the icons of our hunting camp. Russ had become a true honorary Jolly Boy after hunting with us for almost thirty years and was always a complete and enthusiastic participant in the hunting camp right up to his end. He was an excellent hunter, and his game of choice at the poker table was "deuces wild." He had cherished our camp traditions and the fellowship and honor of being a part of our group at Blue Heaven, and we were blessed to have had him as a part of the hunting camp.

There were more changes to our hunting camp group during this period. Ollie's brother-in-law at that time, Nate, began hunting with us during deer season 1997, and Ollie's close friend Brian Lane also became involved in our group. Although we were rapidly losing many of the camp elders, younger and more energetic hunters were now filling the vacated bunks and learning about the traditions and rules that applied to our beloved hunting camp. My partner Dennis and I were beginning to realize that we were now becoming the camp elders, even though we didn't necessarily want that honor.

As the end of the decade approached, the shack log records the fact that our group was beginning to see the fruits of all the younger hunters hunting out of the camp each fall. In 1999, we harvested four deer. Even though we had seven either-sex permits, we decided not to shoot any more deer that year because the weather that season was very warm, with daytime temperatures reaching into the mid-60s. We didn't want to chance having any of the meat spoil. We already had deer waiting to be cut up and put into coolers on ice due to the warm weather, and we didn't want to have any of our coveted venison to spoil. In 1999, we harvested six bucks. The deer herd appeared to be in great abundance, and we had multiple either-sex permits that had not yet been filled, but we had taken the deer we needed, and all agreed not to shoot any more deer unless it was a trophy buck. Deer season 2000 was a repeat of 1999, and we had seven deer hanging on the deer rack outside. Once again, we decided that we had all the venison we needed and that we would allow the remaining deer herd in our area to be left undisturbed.

Hopefully, this would allow the herd to perpetuate itself and assure successful deer seasons in the coming years. The Jolly Boys had taught us well. Harvest only what you need for your own use. Respect nature and what it has to offer. Never get overly greedy so that you will make sure you will have deer in your area for the coming years and generations.

DEER SEASON 1996 CAMP LOG ENTRIES

Volume II of our shack log provides very specific details of the 1996 deer season at Blue Heaven. The entries are very representative of most deer seasons and I quote directly from the log to provide the flavor of what actually happens during a typical nine day deer hunt:

Friday 11/23/96 - John, Dennis, Russ, Barry & Bobby arrive about 3 p.m. via Coot to open camp. Road is frozen and in good shape. About 3"of snow on ground. Everyone gets busy putting away supplies and John asks Russ, "Where are the 50 pounds of the 'Best Yet' potatoes you bought in Exeland?" Russ checks all his pockets, turns pale, and begins staring at floor. Dennis puts on coat and makes two hour trip to Russ' house on Chief Lake to pick up 50# of potatoes. Billie-Bob arrives at 4:30 via his new but used '93 Ford Ranger 4X4 with optional pizza cutter tires and heated rear bumper. Dennis Skare is also in attendance checking out the movement into deer camp. Skare leaves to buy deer license and blaze orange equipment and promises to return on Sunday to hunt. Violet's meatballs, boiled rutabaga's and Russ' "well-traveled" potatoes for supper. All settle down about 11 p.m. to rest for opening day only to be awakened by Ollie and Robin arriving at 2 a.m. via noisy Dodge 4X4. Robin arrived twin cities on Sun Country charter at 10:30 p.m. to ride up with Ollie. Ollie brings along two Minnesota deer killed on recent trip to Boundary Waters in northern Minnesota during the Minnesota deer season. Two deer are hanging from the deer pole and no one has even loaded a rifle yet!

*Saturday 11/23/96 – Eight sleepy hunters stumble into woods attempting to fill meat rack. We have four either-sex permits. **** hits fan while Ollie is at "The Birch" and Ollie slays one of four deer and wounds another. Large doe is added to meat rack and attempt is made to track down wounded deer after pancake, egg and sausage breakfast. Appears wounded deer has minor leg wound and although John and Ollie get close, deer escapes all attempts to issue a final blow. Merle makes several calls on camp phone from highway requesting updates on the hunt. All enjoy ribs, kraut and best traveled potatoes for dinner.*

Sunday 11/24/96 – Another attempt is made to track down Ollie's wounded deer with no success. John meets up with Darrell Slama and daughter Rachel from "Club 27" while hunting and both stop in to see Blue Heaven and enjoy a refreshment. Merle calls and Rachel answers camp phone explaining she is new dancing girl. Merle hangs up phone very confused thinking he dialed wrong number. Dennis Skare arrives sporting new blaze orange hunting outfit, his first Wisconsin deer license and carrying borrowed rifle from Merle. Skare is posted by horse barn where he proceeds to contaminate the woods and his new hunting outfit after over-indulging on eggs at breakfast. Skare leaves deer camp after his two hour hunt grumbling that no one should be allowed to have this much fun. DNR special contamination team is brought in to decontaminate Birch Street. Rob and Ollie are fed Violets left-over meatballs with shack peas for supper as they have to return to twin cities. Rest of us dine on spaghetti and garlic French bread later. Dennis and Barry have marathon dish washing event. Billie-Bob wins all the money at the poker game.

Monday 11/25/96 – Weather is turning colder. Highs in the teens and lows are sub-zero. Lots of fresh sign below The Birch and by the Horsebarn but no more deer. Billie-Bob picks up Adder and Merle at 5 p.m. for their visit to camp. Served Shack Steak made with Ollie's Minnesota deer along with potatoes and Shack Peas for dinner following a fun game of poker where Barry and John win all the money. Monday morning had been spent cutting up one of Ollie's deer and starting the pot of vegetable beef soup. Had Violets left-over meatballs over bread for brunch.

Tuesday 11/26/96 – Clear and cold. Mid-teens for the

*daytime high. Quite a bit of deer sign but still no new deer. Bobby spends much of afternoon "sipping" and quickly becomes Mr. El-Blasto by early evening. Lester Schaaf arrives late p.m. to partake in festivities and loses deer rifle and pickup in poker game. (Only kidding.) Appears Lester spent much of p.m. having a few to take the edge off as he's Mr. Smiley on arrival in camp. Left-over spaghetti for supper with Italian salad and garlic toast. Dennis and Billie-Bob play guest chefs in shack kitchen and made several ****-ups in the attempt. Lester is given sponge bath by Dennis to clean off spaghetti on hands and face and then steered into center middle bunk via Adder's Ladder. Very obvious to all that the drunk fairy made a visit to Blue Heaven and tapped her magic wand on Bobby and Lester. Bobby wins all the money and once again declares "first time ever" win of show-down game. Rest of evening spent attempting to clean table cloth around Lester's plate.*

Wednesday 11/27/96 – Everyone departs for Thanksgiving except for Dennis, Russ and Barry. Dinner of left-over Shack Steak, meatballs, potatoes and Shack Peas. Barry wins all the money in poker game.

Thursday 11/28/96 – Barry leaves camp leaving Dennis and Russ alone for Thanksgiving dinner which Barbara had brought out to them. Both spend day doing a little hunting and taking care of many chores around camp including the skinning and cutting up of one of Ollie's Minnesota deer. Ollie and his friend Brian Lane return to camp about 2 a.m.

Friday 11/29/96 – Merle makes inspection trip to camp and returns to town after a cup of coffee. Bobby, Billie-Bob and John arrive later in a.m. Left-over vegetable soup for brunch. Derrik pays visit to camp and stays for snacks and poker game. Russell wins all the money and declares Derrik his favorite gaming person after Derrik contributes heavily to Russ' winnings. We dine on probably the best venison loins ever along with Shack Green Beans and potatoes. Weather has warmed and brought rain which turns to snow that is sticking to everything. Brian "camp houseboy" Lane wins show-down game.

Saturday 11/20/96 – Everyone, except our houseboy, goes out for the hunt in woods wet with snow that has stuck to everything. Several hot tracks are followed with no luck. Russ gets a shot at a deer and Bobby sees a deer and immediately returns to camp to start celebrating. Four pounds of bacon, blueberry pancakes and eggs for brunch. Afternoon is spent cutting up Ollie's big doe shot at The Birch. Poker game lasting until 10 p.m. followed by venison loins served with green pepper, mushrooms and onions and shack baked potatoes. Ollie becomes exhausted and sneaks into his bunk at 9:15 and misses supper. John wins the final show-down game.

(L-R) Marv Hanson prepares brunch while John "JK" Dunster and his friend Ward Williamson enjoy a beer in the early days of Blue Heaven.

"JK"'s old 1966 Willy's CJ5 Jeep after it was rebuilt by Ollie Hanson: new wheels and over-sized tires, new paint, running lights and a H.D. winch.

Lunch Fare

There's probably nothing more satisfying for a noon lunch during deer camp when it's cold and windy outside than a hearty bowl of soup or stew. After the first few days of deer camp, most of us get tired of the traditionally huge lumberjack style of breakfast involving eggs with breakfast meat and wanted to have a more traditional meal when we arrived back at camp for our noon break. Accordingly, these two camp favorites started to become a part of our lunch tradition.

VEGETABLE BEEF SOUP WITH DUMPLINGS

Vegetable beef soup with dumplings is always a big hit. We always make a huge pot of it so there is an ample amount for leftovers with saltines and plenty of butter. This recipe will serve 6-8 hungry hunters for at least two meals.

Ingredients:

3- or-4-lb. pot roast (purchase an inexpensive cut of beef roast. Don't bother with soup bones. There's no meat on soup bones!)

1 large yellow onion

½ stalk celery

1 2-lb. package carrots

1 large rutabaga

3 large potatoes

Beef bouillon (use the paste type, not beef broth or beef bouillon cubes)

Salt and pepper

Preparation:

Begin by taking a large kettle, one that will hold about three gallons of water. Fill the kettle about half full with water and bring to a simmer. Put the pot roast into the water and add about 2 tablespoons of beef bouillon paste, a half tablespoon of salt, and a half tablespoon of black pepper. (Don't oversalt the broth, because the beef bouillon has an intense salt flavor also.) Slice up a half-stalk of celery into pieces that are about a quarter-inch wide, and dice up the yellow onion and add to the pot. Simmer for about three or four hours until the pot roast becomes falling-apart tender. Sample the broth after it has simmered for a couple of hours to determine whether more salt or beef bouillon is needed. If so, add additional salt or bouillon to taste. If overly salty, simply add more water to the pot to dilute.

Once the pot roast is cooked, pull it from the broth and put it on a plate. Remove any fat from the roast and then use a fork to shred the roast by pulling the fork through the meat. Discard fat, and put the shredded pot roast back into the pot, and continue to simmer.

Peel and dice the rutabaga into small cubes about a half-inch wide and add to the pot. Rutabaga takes a long time to cook, so this should be added to the broth for simmering about 45 minutes before adding the carrots and potatoes.

Peel and cut the two pounds of carrots into half-inch slices and add to the pot. Peel and dice the potatoes into cubes about a half-inch in width and add them to the pot. Allow this mixture to simmer until all of the vegetables become very tender.

Once the soup is fully cooked and the broth has passed your taste test, it's time to make the dumplings. Make certain that there is ample broth in the pot, since dumplings will soak up a lot of the broth as they are cooking. Dumplings are very easy to make, and they will add a dimension of heartiness to the soup.

DUMPLINGS

Measure out three cups of all-purpose flour and put in a mixing bowl. Stir in one teaspoon of salt. Beat up four eggs in a separate cup. Add the eggs to the flour and salt and mix thoroughly. Quickly add two cups of boiling water to the mixture and stir rapidly to prevent the eggs from turning into scrambled eggs. The mixture will be the consistency of a heavy paste. Bring the soup to a moderate rolling boil and use a spoon to drop the dumpling mixture into the boiling soup broth, alternating the positioning of the dumplings so they don't stick together. Once the dumplings have been deposited in the broth, cover the soup kettle with a lid and allow them to cook in the moderately boiling broth for about 15 minutes. As the dumplings cook, they will float to the surface of the soup, and the dumpling mixture will actually double or triple in size.

Put the entire pot on the table, using pot holders or a cutting board to protect the table top from the heat of the pot. Use a ladle to serve the soup in large soup bowls, and serve to your hungry hunters with lots of saltines and butter.

The dumplings will all be consumed during the first serving of this lunch favorite, so be prepared to mix up another batch of dumplings when the leftover soup is served on another day!

VENISON STEW

Another noontime hit with all of our hungry hunters is venison stew. This can be made with either fresh venison or venison steak that is already cooked and has been left over from a previous dinner. It's also an excellent way to use any venison left over from a previous deer season that's been sitting in your freezer and is starting to get old. This recipe will feed 6-8 people and is wonderful served with warmed buns and lots of butter.

Ingredients:

3 to 4 lbs. venison round steak cut from the hind quarter of the deer and cubed into bite-sized portions about ¾-1 inch.

¼ lb. Parkay or a similar product

1 large yellow onion

1 2-lb. package carrots

4 large potatoes

Beef bouillon (use the paste type, not beef broth or bouillon cubes)

1 tablespoon prepared horseradish

3 bay leaves

Salt and pepper

Flour, corn starch, or Wondra Flour

Water

Preparation:

After cutting the venison into cubes and trimming off any tallow or fat, place the cubes in large frying pan with the stick of Parkay. Brown all sides of the venison on moderate heat, stirring frequently. (If leftover venison is being used, simply heat the venison in the Parkay without allowing it to overcook.) Dice the onion into large pieces and add to the venison while it is still frying. Liberally salt and pepper the venison and onion. Once the venison and onion mixture has been browned, transfer it to a kettle, cover the mixture with water, and bring it to a simmer. Add a tablespoon of beef paste and blend it in. Put in the bay leaves and 1 tablespoon of horseradish. Cover the kettle and allow to simmer for one to two hours.

While the venison stew is simmering, peel the carrots and potatoes and dice them into cubes about ¾” to one inch in bite-sized pieces. Place the carrots and potatoes into a pot with salted water and boil them until they are tender. Once tender, drain and add the carrots and potatoes to the stew. Add additional water, if needed, to cover all ingredients. Simmer for an additional half-hour and then thicken the liquid in the stew by taking equal parts of water and flour or water and corn starch, and shaking the mixture in a container to remove lumps. Bring the stew up to a hard simmer and slowly add the thickening agent to the stew broth to thicken the gravy to your preferred consistency. (One can also use a product called Wondra Flour, which is a pre-sifted flour used for thickening sauces. If Wondra is used, simply shake the flour into the beef broth while it is simmering heavily, stirring constantly until the preferred consistency has been obtained.)

Remove the bay leaves and serve the stew in large soup bowls along with fresh bakery buns and lots of butter. Have the salt and pepper shakers handy for anyone who prefers additional seasoning.

2001-2003

Although the deer season in the fall of 2000 proved to be unusually warm, Mother Nature did a turnabout shortly afterward. Because of numerous snowstorms, we were all getting concerned about the snow load on the aging shack roof, as there had been many reports of roofs collapsing under the weight of the snow. Several members of our hunting camp went into the shack by snowmobile to shovel off the roof, which had almost three feet of snow on it. They also installed a brace inside the shack to help support the roof in the event this weather pattern continued. The building was now 45 years old, and time and previous harsh winters had made the roof a swayback. It was always a cause for concern.

Deer season 2001 also brought with it unusually warm weather. We had shot two bucks on opening morning of deer season, placing a tarp tent over the buck pole to keep the deer out of the sun. By the first Tuesday of that season, we once again had seven deer hanging from the buck pole and once again declared that any additional deer would be only a trophy buck situation. That season, there was considerable conversation during our evening poker games about

Chronic Wasting Disease (CWD), which had been discovered in the deer population in the southern part of the state. Although none of the deer in our area had been diagnosed with CWD, we were still all very concerned, because the jury was still out on whether the venison being consumed was safe to eat. As a result, we made the decision to discontinue our practice of eating pickled venison heart and fried venison liver. As a precaution, we also started to wear rubber gloves when dressing out the deer taken during the hunt.

The following deer season in 2002 saw only the younger hunters showing up for the hunt. None of the "camp elders" were in attendance that year. Bobby had elected not to attend deer camp, as he was coping with a bad knee and felt it in his best interests to stay home. The conversations at the table during this season primarily concentrated on the future of our deer camp for our generation and generations to come. There had been many talks between Sawyer County Board members and the Sawyer County Forestry Department about the possibility of discontinuing the recreational use permits in that county. Deep down, we knew that that decision was inevitable. Surrounding counties had already made the decision to discontinue the permits, and it was only a matter of time before Sawyer County would do the same. Much discussion followed concerning options for our group, including purchasing a small portion of land nearby to which we could move Blue Heaven. A decision was made that we would all explore what might be available in the area, and discussions were also held on how to dismantle and move the building once a new location had been found. In March of 2003, I wrote a letter to the Sawyer County Board and the Sawyer County Forestry Department outlining the importance of the hunting camps to the 100 permit holders and encouraging them to continue with the practice of the recreational use permits. The following month, my mother, Violet, the last surviving Jolly Girl, passed away at the age of 85. It was becoming very evident that the end of the era of the "Greatest Generation" was coming more rapidly than any of us wanted to admit.

Deer season 2003 started out very slowly but ended up very successfully. Opening weekend was warm, with no snow on the ground. However, that all changed on Monday, when it turned colder and we received eight inches of snow. The new snow generated a great deal of excitement, and that afternoon Brian Lane shot two large eight-point bucks and a large doe at the Ravine. We were able to harvest three more deer that season, thanks to the snow on the ground. We also tried a new recipe up at camp that year. Ollie had been in South Dakota that fall and brought to camp eight pheasants that he had shot. Normally, our menu at deer camp avoided poultry, such as chicken. Because Thanksgiving always fell during deer hunting week, everyone filled up on turkey. That year, however, we made an exception and experienced some very fine dining with "pheasant under cast-iron," garlic mashed potatoes, and Violet's superb cabbage-apple salad.

"PHEASANT UNDER CAST IRON"

This recipe works equally well for pheasants, partridge, or quail. All have a delicate dry meat which requires slow cooking at low heat in the "gravy" to keep the meat moist. This recipe serves eight.

Ingredients:

8 birds which have been split in half, washed, and had any birdshot removed.

¼ lb. (1 stick) butter

2 cans cream mushroom soup or 3 cans Dawn Fresh Mushroom Sauce

2 cups half & half

1 large can mushroom stems & pieces

Salt & pepper

Preparation:

Cut the pheasants, partridge, or quail in half lengthways and place them in a non-stick frying pan after slowly melting the butter. Salt and pepper the birds to taste. Slowly fry the birds on both sides until lightly browned. While the birds are frying, use a saucepan and mix the mushroom soup or mushroom sauce, along with the half & half and the can of mushrooms. Slowly heat the mixture but do not bring to a simmer. When the birds are brown and the gravy is warmed, place the birds in a cast-iron Dutch oven. If a Dutch oven is not available, use a regular roasting pan. We use the Dutch oven in the wood cook stove at deer camp, but a regular roasting pan is also suitable. Pour the gravy mixture over the birds, and cover the pan tightly while the birds are cooking to keep them as moist as possible. If your lid doesn't fit tightly, use aluminum foil to seal. Cook in the oven at 275 to 300 degrees for about two hours.

GARLIC MASHED POTATOES

Garlic mashed potatoes are as easy to make as regular mashed potatoes. Naturally, the secret ingredient is garlic. Use an ample amount. We take two whole bulbs of garlic cloves and cut off the root end. We then saturate the bulbs with olive oil and wrap them in aluminum foil. The garlic can then be roasted in the oven along with the birds. Just prior to serving dinner, using a mixer or a potato masher, mash up your boiled potatoes along with about a cup of milk, a quarter pound of butter, and the cooked garlic. Add the garlic bulbs by removing them from the foil and squeezing the cooked garlic cloves out of their skins into the potatoes.

VIOLET'S CABBAGE-APPLE SALAD

Ingredients:

1 small head of cabbage
1 cup Miracle Whip salad dressing
1 tablespoon sugar
2 Red Delicious apples

Cut up the cabbage into coleslaw-sized pieces and place in a large mixing bowl. Core the apples, chop into small pieces, and add to the cabbage. (Always use Red Delicious apples. Other apples are too tart!) Add the salad dressing to the cabbage, sprinkling it with the sugar. Blend all ingredients and chill. More salad dressing and sugar can be added if needed.

Serve the birds and gravy over the garlic mashed potatoes and use the salad as a side dish. One could easily substitute wild rice for the mashed potatoes, but one would then miss out on all that wonderful gravy in which the birds have been cooking!

Financing the Operation of a Hunting Camp

One of the key elements to the success of a hunting camp is to pay the bills connected with its operation while at the same time making the experience affordable. The Jolly Boys had developed a per diem charge when they established Blue Heaven. Each hunter was assessed $5.00 per day to cover the costs of groceries, beer, supplies, taxes, insurance, and permit fees. Naturally, these costs continued to escalate over the years. By the late 1990s, we were charging $25.00 per day and even that fee did not fully cover the expenses. The recreational use permit was now costing us $500.00 per year plus an additional $500.00 per year. The latter amount was being placed in escrow to help defray the costs of removal of the camps of those who chose to simply walk away when their permit was discontinued. Accordingly, at a meeting during deer season 2002, we all agreed that the daily fee would increase to $30.00 to cover the costs of food and other supplies. Each hunter who was a regular member of our group would pay an additional $150.00 per year to cover the fixed costs of taxes, insurance, and the recreational use permit. We agreed that this was fair for all and necessary to keep our financial situation solvent. Everyone who hunted up there knew that there was no profit being realized from what was being charged. We all felt that what we were being charged per season was still a bargain, given all the great food we were consuming and the accommodations that were being afforded. At the end of each deer season, the camp checkbook would be down to the bare bones except for a few hundred dollars left in the account for emergencies. This became a problem as we began to discuss the possibilities of purchasing land somewhere to move the camp should the county eliminate the recreational use permits.

THE RICE LAKE HUNTING TRAGEDY

Deer season 2004 was a huge success. We harvested a ten-point buck, an eight-point, a six-point, and two spike bucks, along with four large does. This was the most deer ever taken out of our hunting camp during deer season, and we rejoiced in our good fortune. That deer season would be remembered for a senseless tragedy in the Rice Lake area. An out-of-state hunter from Minnesota got into an argument with several hunters who had a camp where he decided to hunt near Rice Lake, and the argument turned violent. The Minnesota hunter shot and killed five of the hunters from that camp and wounded three others. One of the wounded also died later that week. Every deer hunter in Wisconsin was outraged over this event, and there was a huge outpouring of donations that were sent to a bank in Rice Lake to assist the families of the victims. To this day, no one can understand why this happened.

ELIMINATION OF THE RECREATIONAL USE PERMITS

Shortly after deer season 2004, we received a letter from Mike Krueger, Forest Administrator for Sawyer County. He advised us that he thought the cabins on county forest lands would be safe until 2011, but there were no assurances that the county board would approve extending the permits beyond that date.

This was followed by a huge county board meeting on 11/01/04, with over 125 people in attendance voicing their opinions on the camp permit issues. Sawyer County was the only county in the state without a phase-out plan for the permits. Washburn County had only 35 remaining cabins, and there were only 12 permits in Polk County, with six or seven permits left in Rusk and Clark Counties. The Sawyer County Board was very concerned that if they continued to issue the permits against the will of the DNR, they could potentially lose substantial timber revenue from the county forest lands.

By January of 2005, there was substantial discussion about possibly obtaining an outside legal opinion regarding the legality of the permits, but most county board members opposed using taxpayer money to hire an attorney. The board knew they were under the gun to develop a new ten-year comprehensive forest-management plan, and it was becoming very obvious that the camp permits would not be a part of that plan.

Worried about the non-renewal of our camp permit in the not-too-distant future and knowing we were in charge of our own destiny concerning Blue Heaven, I wrote a letter to Darrell Slama. He was one of the owners of Club 27, a hunting camp about a mile to the west of our current location. Darrell and several other men owned 36.37 acres of land, and their deer camp was just on the opposite side of the highway in the northwest portion of their property. The majority of their land was on our side of the highway, and we decided it would be ideal if they sold us enough land in the southwest corner of their acreage to relocate our hunting camp. My lengthy letter to Darrell outlined in great detail the dilemma with which we were confronted. I enclosed copies of the numerous articles that had been written in local papers, along with a copy of a plat map indicating the portion of their property we wished to purchase. I also enclosed several copies of my correspondence so Darrell could share my proposal with the other members of Club 27.

About a week after I sent my letter to Darrell in January of 2005, Sawyer County joined the other 28 counties in Wisconsin that had agreed to discontinue private hunting camps on county land. There had been an enormous amount of confusion over the interpretation of the law under Wisconsin State Statute 28.11, and the county board felt that hiring an attorney to explore this law further was not feasible, given the fact that Sawyer County was the only county in the state still allowing the permits. The Sawyer County Board voted 12-3 to end the permits, and the sunset date for the removal of the hunting camps from Sawyer County forest lands was set at 12/31/10. We were devastated at this decision. We realized that we had only five short years in which to locate property, move the camp, and re-establish it at the new location if we wanted to keep Blue Heaven from becoming just a memory.

From that point forth, every time we got together, the topic of conversation would be about available options. Ollie had purchased a 40-acre plot of wild land several miles to our north, which was given heavy consideration. However, that location was too far away to allow us to hunt the hallowed hunting grounds on which we had been hunting for the past 50 years. We needed to find something closer, because no one wanted to hunt anywhere except where we were currently hunting. It was sacred to us, so much so that Dennis had even spread a portion of his father's ashes in an area where Russ used to spend late afternoons hunting while sitting on the side of a hill overlooking a swamp and watching the sun set behind the hemlock pine trees. This area was familiar to us, and we had honored it for half a century, giving names to the logging roads and landmarks within the area. We even considered moving the shack onto a mobile home trailer and taking the shack back to that location for deer season every year. Unfortunately, the logistics of that plan seemed too complicated to make it practical. We also checked with all the local realtors, asking them to try to locate a nearby parcel of land for us. None was to be had, and the local property owners did not appear to have much interest in selling any of their property. Ultimately, we all decided that our best option would be to try to convince Club 27 to sell us a few acres in the southeast corner of their land. It was within a quarter mile of our present location and would be ideal.

2005–Blue Heaven's 50th Anniversary

On Friday, November 18, 2005, we all gathered to go to deer camp to celebrate our 50th year at the hunting shack. It had been quite a feat. The Jolly Boys' dream had perpetuated itself for five decades and the camp was still going strong. Many things had changed over the years, but it seemed that the more they changed, the more they had stayed the same. We were all very proud that our camp was still intact after all these years, and a party to celebrate the event certainly was in order.

We were greeted at the camp by four inches of new snow on the ground and a coating on all of the trees. The woods were beautiful. Although there weren't many fresh deer tracks in the area, there was an abundance of wolf tracks as well as signs that a bear or two were still wandering around, not yet settled in for their long winter's nap. That night, we dined on huge plates of Reali spaghetti and French bread garlic toast. A Caesar's salad had been on the menu but not made, as someone had eaten all the anchovies with the rest of the snacks that had been put out beforehand, and one couldn't possibly enjoy a Caesar's salad without an ample amount of anchovies. The temperature was ideal—in the low 30s—and every hunter was settled in his bunk by 11 p.m. to get a good night's rest before the season opener the next morning.

We spent many hours in the woods on Saturday, but no one saw any deer. It was very disappointing to have been "skunked" on the season opener. Sunday was a different story. Ollie shot two large does from his tree stand at the Birch early that morning, and Dennis bagged a spike buck soon afterward to give himself a birthday present. His birthday fell during deer season every year, and he had spent most of the day mumbling something about "a birthday buck." We purposely quit hunting early that day to return to the shack to prepare for our 50th anniversary party. Merle, the last surviving Jolly Boy, and Bobby Hanson arrived at 4 p.m. to join us in the celebration via the Coot driven by Dennis. Both were having difficulties ambulating, along with other assorted health issues, but neither would have missed this party. Bobby was eager to get the poker game "afoot," and Merle had pulled out several old photo albums to share the memories of the good old days at Blue Heaven. Merle also brought in anniversary hats that he had made for everyone to wear, and Rob produced special T-shirts he had secretly ordered for everyone. A vast array of snacks was set out for everyone to enjoy during the card game. In the old cook stove, I prepared a huge, succulent, medium-rare bone-in prime rib roast heavily encrusted with an olive oil/crushed garlic topping, along with garlic mashed potatoes and a salad loaded with homemade blue cheese dressing and blue cheese crumbles. It was a meal fit for a king, and we all wished that all the Jolly Boys of old could have been in attendance for this special occasion. There had been considerable discussion that evening while we were playing cards about possibly purchasing some land from Club 27 when the recreational use permits expired. Very content, Merle and Bobby left camp that evening about 8 p.m. Neither one was in physical condition to spend any overnights at camp any longer. We drove them back to town to make certain that they arrived home safely. It was very sad to watch them drive out of sight on that old logging road after that party. We all knew that, in all probability, that evening would be the last time either of them would be at the hunting camp they both loved so much.

November 20, 2005. Merle Dunster, the last surviving "Jolly Boy," makes his final trip to "Blue Heaven" to celebrate the 50th Anniversary of the deer camp. Merle is sitting at his usual place at the table, playing his favorite game of poker, sipping on a brandy "Manhattan" which was his favorite drink, and reminiscing about the days of old while I shuffle the cards preparing to deal the next game. An array of snacks are on the kitchen counter, a 12 lb. prime rib roast is slowly cooking in the wood burning stove behind us, and we are all sporting our "Camp 52–Blue Heaven" T-shirts in celebration of the event. It was an evening to remember.

THE FINAL DEER SEASONS AT BLUE HEAVEN

The mood was very different in the final deer seasons at the old hunting shack. The fact that we were losing the camp was always in the back of everyone's mind, and it was reflected every day we spent up there. Plans had to be made to pack up everything, and a plan would have to be made as to where to store the contents of the shack until a new location could be found. It would be a major undertaking, and the uncertainty of our future was the only thing dampening our spirits during these last few seasons at the old shack.

On the first morning of deer season 2006, the light plant was fired up at 3:30 a.m., to everyone's shock and dismay. Someone from the bunk area yelled, "Don't ya think you're getting a little anxious?!" As it turns out, Ollie had set his alarm clock incorrectly, having been off by about an hour and a half. The light plant was turned off and, traumatized by the experience, we all finally drifted back to sleep until almost 6 a.m.

There was lots of deer sign in the woods on Saturday but no deer were seen. On Sunday, Rob shot a spike buck at the Big Rock and almost simultaneously, I shot a five-point buck by the Little Rocks. These shots could be heard by the other hunters. There was much debate about who had the rights to the buck money for the first buck taken, but one of our hunters had been posted between the two of us and confirmed that Rob had indeed shot first. We had another successful season that year, harvesting a total of seven deer. Naturally, there were more discussions about the future of the hunting shack, but no decisions had yet been reached.

We had a super deer season in 2007, shooting a camp record nine deer that year. Although we disliked the thought of possibly having to give up our hallowed hunting grounds, Ollie's 40 acres several miles north was beginning to look like our only option.

Things really looked up for us during deer season 2008 when my cousin, Brian Hanson, met one of the Club 27 hunters in the woods. His nickname was "Beach," and he told Brian that members of Club 27 had met and decided that they were willing to sell us a portion of their property for us to relocate our camp, although they needed to find replacement property before doing so to avoid any capital gain taxes on the sale of their property to us (because their camp was incorporated, the sale would have tax consequences unless they located replacement property). Brian returned to camp that afternoon with this great news, knowing that this would be the perfect solution to our problem. The weather that deer season was excellent, and we ended up taking three bucks and three large does.

The only thing that overshadowed the season was the fact that the last of our Jolly Boys, Merle Dunster, had been admitted to a nursing home, as his health was deteriorating and he was no longer capable of caring for himself.

One of the final deer seasons at Old Blue. Enjoying drinks and poker after a day of hunting are the seven regulars at Blue Heaven during deer season. (L-R) Me; my partner, R.D. Clagett; my younger son, Oliver; his friend Mike Schaaf; my cousin, Brian Hanson; my friend Barry Rice; and my older son, Robin.

End of an Era

There was no "fall frolic" in the fall of 2009. It was decided that there was no point in cutting firewood or making any repairs to the shack, because it appeared that deer season 2009 would be the last season we would be able to hunt out of Blue Heaven. We were still trying to conclude a deal with Club 27 to acquire enough of their land to relocate the shack, but that was still uncertain. Our back-up plan was to move the shack to my younger son's 40 acres some six miles north of our current location. My older son was aggressively leading negotiations with the members of Club 27 who still had some concerns over the sale.

When deer season 2009 arrived, the mood was decidedly different. My wife, Kathy, who was a staff reporter for the *Sawyer County Record* newspaper in Hayward, had written a column about our deer camp for the paper which was published shortly after the 2009 deer season. She had listened to all the bemoanings, complaints, and expressions of disappointment about the loss of Blue Heaven. That column drew many comments from readers, some of whom had never hunted deer. Her words had evoked the traditions, love, and nostalgia of our deer hunting camp and had brought tears to the eyes of many readers. The column is framed and hangs above my desk in Hayward.

Goodbye 'Blue Heaven,' we will miss you
Published: Thursday, December 3, 2009 3:11 PM CST
Kathy Hanson
staff reporter

Once again this November, I bore witness to my husband John readying for the deer hunt. It is a long, laborious and protracted procedure, this getting ready for the hunt, and I have grown familiar with the preparations that go into it.

I have also, through the years, grown weary with the preparations that go into it.
It begins in our house about a month before opening day. The guys from the deer camp send their checks to John, who acts as the camp bookkeeper. For the next 30 days, John lines his den with boxes of gear and essentials. Old flannel pillowcases and mismatched sheets, hunting clothing I see only once a year, polished guns, shirts that hold dear memories for him that are lost on me--all are reverently brought out for the hunting season. The revered shack log— where entries dating back to the 1950s record the weather, the hunt, the kill and who lost most at poker— is carefully packed. Numerous lists of ingredients for the artfully-planned menus for every meal, starting with opening day and ending with the Sunday after Thanksgiving, are planned down to the last garlic clove. These meals are not hastily put together, nor are they cheap. There are 50-year old traditions that call for ribs and kraut on a certain evening; prime rib on another and Reali spaghetti made with pork ribs the next night. I could fill an entire column about the meals and you would ask for those recipes, but that isn't what I want to say here.

This year is different because it is the last time my husband and his friends will hunt on their beloved county land with the old shack still standing. The provision to allow cabin permit holders on county forest land has come to an end. On January 26, 2005, the Sawyer County Record reported that the Sawyer County Board of Supervisors voted 12 to three to "discontinue the practice of permitting private hunting cabins on county forest land." And they established the date to end the practice as no later than December 31, 2010.

There's probably no end to the list of good reasons why that had to happen, but it changed the lives and traditions of a lot of lives—at least the 100 cabin permit holders—including my husband's "Blue Heaven" Camp 52, which has been nestled in the Sawyer County Forest since 1955 when his father, Marv Hanson, built it along with the other four original "Jolly Boys:" Adder Madson, Merle Dunster, Kenneth Sugrue and Howard Nystrom. Those Jolly Boys shared that part of the county forest with other hunting camps now folding too—Camp No Hunt, Camp Handicap, Dynamite Hill and Bare Naked Purgatory Swamp—names steeped in shared history and humor.

The night before John left for camp, the living room was filled with his tightly packed army duffel bag, the familiar vintage suitcase, the boxes of spirits and canned goods and the leftover Halloween candy. When I came home from work at 5:30 p.m., I asked him if he didn't want to leave right then. The preparations were so obviously ready that they called out to me, "I can hardly wait to get there."

And I admit that every year I feel a jealous tug as that camp—like nothing else in our life together—completely takes over John's mind and psyche. He reminds me of my younger brothers when I was a kid, and how they awaited Christmas morning so they could open the gifts. It is sheer, unbridled love of the deer camp.

Reprinted with the permisson of the Sawyer County Record

So I was prepared this year to write this column in a humorous vein, pointing out the childish ways and rigid traditions that occupy the minds of the same group of nine or ten grown men who convene up there during what Hayward has dubbed "holy week," a term that would offend all of the nuns who so carefully provided me with a Roman Catholic elementary education in the lives and feasts of all the saints.

Alas, I can't summon up the humor I was so looking forward to sharing. It's gone. As will be the shack and the years and years and years of things done all over again the same way, decade after decade, for the sake and memory of the original Jolly Boys who founded Blue Heaven.

My husband left the house with a heavy heart that Friday morning before opening day. The week would be spent with all of the guys trying to sort out where to build the next shack, what to do with the old shack and its worthless but irreplaceable contents, how to disassemble a shack that holds the memories of births, marriages, grandchildren, deaths and beyond. A shack that one year, shortly after Marvin Hanson died, showed his visage at a window outside during a violent night storm.

As a point of clarification that may not be needed to this reading audience, the hunting camp is really not about the deer, although they are the raison'd'etre for hunting camps like my husband's. It's about tradition. It's about passing the torch. It's about love.

So I will share only one piece of humor that originally was planned for this column. When John comes home for Thanksgiving and then leaves again very early the next morning—always a Friday, of course—he tiptoes up to the bedroom to say goodbye to me. He can't mask the eagerness and the excitement I see in him as he returns to the shack. Even on Thanksgiving Day, as he carves the turkey, his mind is at the shack. I can see it in his eyes and I can hear it in his head, even though he doesn't speak of it. He sits on the side of the bed and I pretend to wake up. He leans over, kisses me and says, "I'm going to mount up."

Yes, that is what he says. The allure and mystery and thrill of the hunt permeates even his language and he imagines himself, I suppose, getting back on his horse to go back into the woods. Year after year, he has said, "I'm going to mount up," and it wasn't until last year that I finally asked him if a horse had replaced his luxury van sitting in the driveway.

But this year was different. He didn't say he was going to mount up. His eyes didn't reflect back the thrill and excitement of the hunt. He seemed subdued, somehow resigned. And I felt his loss. Surely, his father Marvin is not happy about all of this. Nor are John's sons, or his cousin or his other hunting brothers. They are all wondering what happens now. How do we hang on to all those memories contained in the walls of this dilapidated, falling-down, asbestos-shingled camp that has raised us from childhood to boyhood into adulthood and beyond? Where do we go now? Will it ever be the same?

I have no answers, except to say,"mount up" you hunters, and carry those memories and traditions with you as you take your leave of Camp 52. Set up your new camp. Call it Blue Heaven. Make sure young John Dennis Hanson shoots his first buck from that camp, surrounded by all of you who will still be there. Light your fires, play your cards, tell your stories. And look for Marvin in the windows, because he'll be watching.

Deer season 2009 began like most of the deer seasons in prior years. I met Dennis at the area where we parked our vehicles on the Friday before season. The two of us unloaded the Coot from the trailer, loaded it with supplies, and began our trek towards the shack. Rob had hired a surveyor to mark off the boundaries of the southeast corner of the Club 27 property, and the bright orange ribbons marking the property lines were visible as we started to trudge toward the shack. About midway down the well-worn logging road, we stopped the Coot and walked into the woods to see if we could locate the southeast corner stake. It wasn't difficult to find, and we were both very pleased to find that the southeast corner was in the area where we had thought it would be. It was on higher ground, not in a swampy area as we had feared, and there was an excellent building site in a small open area surrounded by tall pine trees. We were eager to tell the others on their arrival. The weather was balmy for November 20, 2009, and the road in to camp was relatively dry. Ollie, Billie-Bob, Mike, and Nate arrived a short time later, followed by Barry. Rob was still in Atlanta studying to take a test for his Master's degree and had to delay his arrival until Sunday. We unloaded and put away the supplies, and I prepared a large batch of church barbeques for our lunch. The afternoon was spent taking care of camp chores and putting up tree stands for opening day the next morning. Our usual poker game with the traditional snacks and beverages was on schedule by 5 p.m., followed by one of our traditional Reali spaghetti dinners. The kitchen was cleaned up, the light plant was turned off, and the candle was lit. We all crawled into our bunks by 11 p.m. to rest up for the big opener.

As I settled into my bunk that had been occupied by my father for so many years, I once again began to soak up all the sounds of the shack that had become so very familiar to me. The antique shack clock was tick-tick-ticking, waiting to sound its loud, obnoxious alarm in the early morning hours. The fire in our old wood cook stove was crackling and still producing ample heat to make the water kettles hiss a little steam. Several of my fellow hunters had already drifted off into slumber, and there was a variety of snoring coming from various parts of the bunk area. It was a peaceful, relaxing, and familiar atmosphere, and I was in disbelief that all of this was coming to an end. I eventually drifted off to sleep with my senses still absorbing everything that was so important to me about that hunting camp.

At 5 a.m., the antique alarm clock went off. The clock never just rang. There would always be several short "dings" before it got into full ringing mode. This was a good thing, as it prepared us for what was to come a few seconds later. As usual, none of us wanted to crawl out of our warm, comfortable bunk, but we all began to stir, as much preparation needed to be accomplished by each of us before we set off into the woods to begin the hunt. It was 25 degrees, and the forecast called for a high around 50 degrees that day.

My cousin, Billie-Bob, shot his first buck, a small deer with spike antlers, in the Little Rocks area. He rushed back to camp to claim the buck money that was attached to the shack wall with an ice pick. Dennis also slew a spike buck on the upper swamp road shortly thereafter, and Nate downed a six-pointer about 10:30 a.m.

Three bucks were hanging from the buck pole. We celebrated our success with Bloody Marys, followed by venison breakfast sausage Billy-Bob had made from the previous season's deer kill, along with pancakes and fried eggs. Several of us saw deer during the afternoon hunt, but no one had a chance for a kill shot. That evening we roasted a 14-pound prime-rib roast to medium-rare perfection in the old wood stove and complemented it with garlic mashed potatoes and Caesar's salad.

Rob arrived from Atlanta at 6 a.m. on Sunday and departed immediately for the Big Rock, where I had seen three deer on opening morning. Ollie shot a doe up by the Can that morning, but deer hunting was difficult, as there was no snow in the woods. We had four deer hanging and were pleased with the results of our hunt thus far.

The remainder of deer season 2009 progressed as usual, with all the good food, the fun poker games, and hunters coming and going throughout the season. After brunch on Monday, Dennis, Rob, Ollie, and I kicked everyone else out of the shack so we could sit down to have a serious discussion among ourselves about the future of the camp when our lease with the county terminated on 12/31/2010. Although we discussed the possibility of hunting from our current location during deer season 2010, we all knew that that would be unrealistic because it would leave us with only a month to vacate after the season was over. If the weather wasn't cooperating, we would be hard-pressed to accomplish everything that needed to be done. We decided that this season would be the last season at the current location. Dennis and I also decided that day to bequeath all of the camp assets to Rob and Ollie, who would become equal partners and the new owners of Blue Heaven. Dennis and I would take on the role of advisors to the two of them but they would be in charge from this point forth. Meanwhile, Rob would conclude a deal with Club 27 to purchase six acres in the southeast corner of their property so we could begin the disassembly and moving of the shack to the new location.

On the final Sunday of the season, we awoke to snow on the ground, too late to do us much good, as it was time to pack up and leave. Breakfast was prepared, and everyone was having somber moments knowing that this day might be the last any of us would be in this hunting camp that had endured since 1955. While we were eating our final meal at the shack, there was much talk of the Jolly Boys of old who would always have one final game of poker before breaking camp on Sunday afternoon and then all congregate with their wives at Gerlach's Landing on Nelson Lake later that day for burgers and tap beer. It was an era with great memories.

The Bloody Marys

Bloody Marys have been a staple at our hunting camp for as long as I can remember. We simply call them "bloodys," and they are never served until late morning during deer camp just prior to our large brunch at noon. As tradition has it, we don't allow bloodys to be served until there is meat hanging from the deer pole. This provides incentive for everyone on the first day of deer season to shoot a deer and get it hanging back at camp before noon so we don't wind up without a bloody to celebrate the hunt.

I've tasted numerous recipes for bloody Marys, most of which are far too spicy for me to enjoy. We make ours slightly on the mild side, and anyone that enjoys a bloody with a kick can certainly add Tabasco sauce, cayenne pepper, or horseradish to their drink if they find them too mild. I give the credit for this recipe to Russ Clagett, who co-owned and operated Herman's Landing for over 25 years and was known for his prowess in putting together a tasty bloody Mary. As Russ said, "Start with your smallest ingredient and work your way up when making a mixed drink." It works.

Use a sizeable glass for the bloody. Something in the 12-18 oz. area works best. Fill the glass about two-thirds full of ice. Add celery salt on top of the ice, shaking the container about 6 to 8 times. Next, add about 4 or 5 large squirts of Worchestershire sauce. Add an ounce and a half of your favorite vodka and a large wedge of lemon that has been squeezed to get as much lemon juice into the drink as possible. Finally, fill the glass with a combination of 50% V-8 Juice and 50% Clamato Juice. Salt and pepper are optional but not really needed. Use a fork to stir thoroughly. Garnish with a beef or celery stick, kosher pickle spear, olives, or whatever you feel is appropriate. Wasn't that easy? Serve with a "snit" of your favorite ice-cold beer. Put out the Tabasco, horseradish and other spices for those who want to burn their lips.

Nine Bloody Mary's prepared at the Bloody Mary bar await nine hunters before sitting down to the late morning brunch. Each glass has the hunter's name written on it to prevent arguments in the event someone misplaces his glass. Each glass contains a venison beer stick to stir all the ingredients.

My partner and second generation owner Russell "Dennis" Clagett, examining a clearing in the southeast corner of the six acres that Club 27 sold us. This field, surrounded by spruce and balsam trees, is where we decided to relocate our beloved Blue Heaven, which was accomplished in the fall of 2010.

Third generation Blue Heaven owners sporting deer season beards Rob Hanson (left) myself (center) and Ollie Hanson (right) toward the end of deer season 2009. It was arranged by Dennis Clagett and myself that Rob and Ollie would "inherit" Blue Heaven when Old Blue was moved and became New Blue.

Overview of the kitchen area and lumberjack table at Blue Heaven taken shortly before the shack was dismantled and moved to the Club 27 property.

Overview of the cabinets and bunk area at Blue Heaven taken shortly before the shack was dismantled.

Movement of Old Blue to New Blue

To ease the transition, Dennis came up with the idea of calling Blue Heaven "Old Blue." So the new camp was named "New Blue." We received Club 27's permission to begin work on the new site in the summer of 2010.

During the winter of 2009-2010, Dennis and I attended multiple meetings with the Town of Lenroot and Sawyer County Zoning to obtain approval for a special-use permit to relocate the camp. On the last weekend of April 2010, Dennis, Ollie, Billie-Bob, Mike, and Brian Lane came to Old Blue for clean-up and disassembly. Rob was in Atlanta working, while Barry was at home recovering from knee surgery. I was out of town that weekend with my wife. The road into camp was bone-dry due to a drought, so transportation wasn't a problem. Ollie built a burn barrel out of an old garbage can, and they began to burn a lot of the junk that had accumulated in the camp over the past 55 years. The shanty was cleaned out, and items that would be needed at the new location were boxed up, including dishes and cooking utensils.

The Playboy centerfolds that had served as decoration in the rafters of the shack for so many years were carefully removed and packed away for safekeeping and possible use at New Blue. Although we had heard rumors that the Sawyer County Board might be considering extending the recreational use permits, we weren't optimistic that that would become a reality, so we proceeded with our plan to relocate. Our goal became to ready the New Blue site and make it habitable by deer season 2010.

Late August gave us a clear and sunny day, with temperatures in the low eighties. There were abundant mosquitoes and deer flies to cope with. We met with Danny Thompson and his brother Mark, of Thompson Sand & Gravel, to lay out and dig footings for New Blue. We decided on the site for the new shack. We then used the 18-inch auger attached to Danny's crawler to dig 15 four-foot holes for the sono tubes. Danny also brought his Bobcat to haul in gravel and a pallet of concrete to fill the sono tubes at a later date.

On September 5, 2010, we received word that the last of the original Jolly Boys, Merle Dunster, had passed away at the Hayward Hospital Nursing Home. The attendance at his funeral was huge, and his attachment to the hunting camp was evident in the photo boards displayed in the narthex of the church. Those in attendance exchanged many fond memories of this icon of Hayward. Merle, along with my father and Adder, had always been the stabilizing force of our hunting camp, and the void that his passing left simply emphasized all of the changes with which we were being confronted as we moved forward to rebuild the camp at the new location.

In mid-September we poured concrete into the 15 sono tubes to serve as support pillars for New Blue. The weather was great, with clear skies and temperatures in the low 60s. We constructed a large box of treated wood which would be placed in a hole in the ground for the new privy to sit on. The next day we poured a concrete slab for the new light plant building in which to house our light plant. We waited a week for the concrete to set and then returned on Friday, September 24, 2010, to haul in lumber for the floor joists and new deck for New Blue. It was a difficult journey to haul in the building supplies. It had rained over two inches, and the road was a mess. We had built a makeshift road through the woods to the new site that quickly turned to a sea of mud with deep ruts and holes, but we were able to wiggle our way in with the aid of winches on the vehicles. We installed the sub-floor that day and then tarped everything to keep the floor from warping in the rain. That evening we returned to Old Blue to spend one last night there before the disassembly process began.

Our last night in Old Blue was memorable. I think that the excitement and anticipation of a new and improved hunting camp negated much of the disappointment we had been feeling, and we awoke Saturday morning to clear skies and a beautiful fall day. We had a quick breakfast. Everyone then went to the New Blue site to finish up a new woodshed, haul the outhouse to the new site, and put up a new buck pole. I stayed behind at Old Blue to empty the cupboards and pack up all of the remaining contents. We all agreed to return on October 8th and 9th to finish the disassembly.

We had finally obtained our building permit, and the big weekend arrived with leafless trees and beautiful weather. The roof was peeled off, and we loaded the unsalvageable debris into a trailer to be hauled to a demolition site. Numerous trips to the dump were necessary to dispose of all the debris and old mattresses. We also discarded the old wood burning cook stove. It had served its purpose and was almost burned out. As we disassembled the shack, we were shocked at the number of mice nests hidden within and the number of wolf spiders that were making their home within the building. Wolf spiders are huge and resemble a tarantula. They scattered, trying to find new shelter as the shack came tumbling down around them. By day's end, Camp 52 was completely disassembled, except for the shanty and shack floor, and was ready to be transported to the new site. Naturally, everyone was exhausted from a day of backbreaking work and ready to head into town for a good night's rest.

On Saturday morning, the entire crew was on-site early. The walls of Old Blue were transported to the new site and installed atop the new subfloor. We were meticulous. We made certain that everything was square and level in the reconstruction process and installed the roof trusses and OSB board that afternoon. New Blue was rapidly taking shape. We ended the day by tarping the roof and temporarily attaching plywood over the window and door openings after hauling the majority of the interior contents to the new building. By 7 p.m. everyone was exhausted and sore but pleased about what had been accomplished. We were on the downhill side of things.

Over the course of the next several weekends, anyone who could make himself available was at New Blue frantically working to get things put back together in anticipation of deer season 2010. Shingles were put on the roof, soffits were installed, electrical wires were run for the lighting, and the boot racks were reinstalled, as was the old oil burner and an updated wood-burning cook stove. The stove pipes were reconnected, and a new asbestos chimney was put in place. We lit the first fires to warm New Blue on October 29, 2010. The kitchen counter and sink were reinstalled, and the plumbing was reconnected. The shelving unit was rehung so we could unload the boxes of dishes and make them accessible. The new shanty was on deadline, so we had an area for storage, but the light plant had to be reinstalled and fired up so we had light at night. There were still many items to be transported from Old Blue to the new site, and the Old Blue site had to be completely cleaned up and void of any debris for inspection by the county in order for us to receive the full refund of several thousand dollars that the county was holding for removal charges in the event they were needed. A portion of our lease payment had been placed in a trust fund each year in the event we abandoned the building and the county had to remove the camp from Sawyer County forest land when our lease terminated. There were many evenings when several of us would simply camp out on the unfinished floor of New Blue, because the new bunk area wasn't completed until November 5, 2010, when we took delivery of nine new designer mattresses. On Sunday, November 7, 2010, the demolition work and removal of debris from Old Blue was completed and Old Blue was no more. By November 13, 2010, there was already half a foot of snow on the ground, so we were relieved that we had completed our mission of moving and reconstructing the new shack with only days to spare before the weather would have made things impossible.

There were still many projects left to be done, but we were all confident that many of these projects could be completed during deer season 2010, which was scheduled to start on November 20, 2010. Except for being four feet wider, the interior of New Blue looked exactly like Old Blue. We were amazed at what we had accomplished in such a short period of time and were looking forward to hunting out of this renovated hunting camp in a couple of weeks.

Brian and Ollie back-filling 12 four-foot deep sono-tubes that were used as pillars to support the floor joists to build the subflooring for New Blue.

The 12 sono-tubes were filled with concrete after being properly spaced and leveled, awaiting appliation of the floor joists for New Blue at the building site.

The contents of Old Blue were removed from shelves and drawers and stored in boxes waiting to be transferred to New Blue. It was a sad time for all of us.

The old worn-out mattresses were removed from the bunk area and the disassembly of Old Blue began by peeling off the shingles, roof boards and rafters.

The asbestos siding was stripped off of Old Blue and hauled to a proper disposal site. All lumber from Old Blue would be salvaged and used in the reconstruction of New Blue. The rotten floor joists and shingles were also taken to the disposal site.

Rob's ATV was used to trailer out debris and garbage from the disassembly.

Mike Schaaf and Ollie Hanson used a small chain saw to cut the walls of Old Blue into eight-foot sections to be transported via trailer and reassembled at New Blue.

By day's end, the only part of Old Blue standing was the previously attached exterior shanty. It was a hard day.

Once the concrete pillars had "cured," the outside framework for the floor joists of New Blue was carefully constructed, assuring it was level and square.

The center beam to support the floor joists was constructed and installed and then secured atop the center concrete pillars.

The "Coot" was used to trailer in the lumber for the floor joists and subfloor on a trail we built to New Blue that was rapidly deteriorating.

The new floor joists were cut and secured in place. The floor joists from Old Blue were too rotted to be used in the construction of New Blue.

Barry Rice held the tape while project manager Ollie Hanson made a final check to ensure the subfloor was level and square, and then drilled the final nails.

Ollie and Barry began to install the subfloor while the rest of us hauled building materials to the job site.

New ceiling trusses were transported by trailer using Ollie's ATV, as the winch on the ATV had to be used frequently to wiggle through the deep muddy ruts.

The eight-foot sections from Old Blue were transported to the building site by trailer and set into place. The reconstruction of New Blue had begun!

Michael and Ollie were meticulous in ensuring the old walls were plumb before they were nailed into place on the new level and square subfloor of New Blue.

Installing the old walls on New Blue went quickly. We decided to reverse the walls, using the old siding as the new interior walls of New Blue in the bunk area.

Mike and Rob installed the walls in the kitchen area and the building was starting to resemble the old hunting shack by the end of the day.

New trusses were installed atop the reconstructed walls of Old Blue as the roof system from the old shack was too decomposed to be salvaged in its entirety.

Mike and Ollie began the process of applying the OSB roof sheathing onto the roof trusses while the rest of us cut the OSB to size.

Sheathing of the roof went quickly. All of us were anxious to finish the roof to enclose the new building to shelter our tools and the contents from Old Blue.

Old Blue has been transitioned into New Blue. Lots of work remained but we could all see the light at the end of the tunnel.

The "road" into New Blue had become a real challenge to maneuver due to numerous trips into the building site from Old Blue and the highway.

Dennis takes a Schlitz break while working on the Kohler light plant which was brought from Old Blue and reset on a new concrete slab.

Ollie makes final adjustments to the framework of the new woodshed to install the new metal roof.

The woodshed at Old Blue was too old and rotted to be salvaged. It was torn down and the yellow birch within was transported to New Blue.

The metal roof system on the new woodshed at New Blue is completed and stacked full of seasoned yellow birch for the upcoming deer season.

The outhouse was transported from Old Blue and set in place according to code. Brian installed a new metal roof of the structure as an upgrade.

After the shingles and stove pipe were installed on New Blue, work began on an attached shanty to house our refrigerators and provide much needed storage.

New Blue

We spent every weekend in the fall of 2010 frantically working to prepare the new hunting camp for the upcoming deer season. One of the priority projects was to complete the framework for the new bunks so we could take delivery of the nine new "designer" mattresses Rob had ordered to replace the 55-year-old mattresses that we had thrown out when dismantling Old Blue. The new mattresses were very thick and firm. They would be a huge improvement over the swayback mattresses and old-fashioned springs on which we had slept for so many years. It took us only a day to complete the project, and every hunter was looking forward to organizing his assigned bunk area by deer season.

It was agreed by all that deer season 2010 would be a combined deer hunt and work party to finish off the interior of New Blue, as there was still considerable interior finishing to be accomplished. The interior of New Blue was still void of finished walls and ceiling, and the flooring still needed to be applied. We would use the salvaged lumber from Old Blue to complete these tasks and would also apply the old tongue-and-grooved maple flooring from Old

Blue over the OSB subflooring. Our goal was to recycle and use as much of the lumber from Old Blue as possible in finishing off the interior. This was being done not only to save on the cost of construction of New Blue but also to retain the history and ambiance of Old Blue. New Blue also required additional weatherproofing, as there were numerous areas that still needed caulk and sealing to help retain heat within the building during the cold nights of deer season. It was decided that we would spend the first weekend of deer season hunting, hoping to get some venison hanging on the new buck pole. We would then devote the majority of the rest of the season to working on the various construction projects.

We arrived at New Blue for deer season 2010. All of us were thrilled over the fact that we had been able to disassemble Old Blue and rebuild Blue Heaven at the new location over the course of the summer and fall of 2010. There was still much to be done, but we had accomplished a great deal, and New Blue was beginning to look just like Old Blue on the interior. We celebrated with a champagne-and-prime-rib dinner on the opening Saturday evening of deer camp, toasting each other for all of the hard work and sacrifices everyone had made to provide us with a new base camp in which to hunt. Although the temperatures only reached the mid-teens during the day and there was snow on the ground, we were relatively comfortable in our new surroundings. There was considerable discussion about the projects remaining to be completed. We were fortunate to harvest five deer that season and considered it a success. We spent many days at camp that year unpacking boxes of dishes and other items that had been moved to New Blue from Old Blue late in the fall. We also returned to the site of Old Blue, as there was enough snow on the ground to burn a pile of scrap lumber unfit for use at New Blue. The former site of Blue Heaven had now been totally cleared of everything and soon would be reclaimed by the forest. Ollie located an old-fashioned Schlitz beer sign and had it cleaned up with new lettering. He had its lights wired to the light plant and installed it on the new buck pole.

After we closed up New Blue at the end of deer season 2010, the camp sat idle through the winter. We returned in the first weekend in April 2011 to find that it had wintered without any problems. Although the temperature was in the mid-50s, there was still a half-foot of snow on the ground. However, that did not deter us from the many projects we wanted to accomplish. Work was done on the roof overhangs to seal up areas prone to critters and bugs attempting to get inside, additional wood was cut up and split for the wood-burning cook stove, and numerous other small projects were tackled in preparation for closing up the camp for the summer months. It was doubtful that any of us would be returning during the summer, as there were simply too many mosquitoes, deer flies, and other bugs to make visiting New Blue a pleasurable experience during the heat of the summer months. Plans were also made to build a bridge across a portion of swamp leading from our parking area into New Blue, as often the swamp was too wet to make maneuvering across it an easy journey. There was much discussion about what needed to be done when we returned in the fall. A priority item was to construct a new light plant building to enclose the light plant that was sitting out in the elements covered by a tarp when not in use.

When we returned that fall, we came loaded with a new, pre-built light plant building, used metal dock sections for the new bridge, and the necessary tools to begin the task of putting down the wood floor and installing wood paneling inside New Blue. Ollie had also located a Jewel wood-burning cook stove to replace our existing stove, which was starting to show signs of the grates and lids "burning out" from many years of use. It was a weekend where much was accomplished. The light plant building was installed atop the concrete pad on which the light plant sat, and the new wood-burning cook stove was installed. Ollie had brought his planer along, and several of us ran all the wood from Old Blue through the planer to clean it up for reinstallation in New Blue. By weekend's end, the maple flooring had been installed, and much of the interior paneling was also adorning the walls. We were no longer thinking of New Blue as a hunting "shack." It was quickly being transformed into a hunting "lodge"!

The new "designer" mattresses arrive via trailer pulled by Rob's ATV. Everyone is anxiously awaiting their installation in the new bunk frames.

The nine new mattresses are installed in the bunk area. Everyone is looking forward to having a place to sleep instead of the unfinished shack floor.

Mike and Ollie stand on top of stepladders installing interior roof boards salvaged from the Old Blue roof and being reused in New Blue. These boards are over 55 years old.

One side of the interior of the roof inside New Blue nears completion. The fan shown in the peak area is used to circulate cigar, cigarette and cooking smoke ... and flatulence.

Mike and Ollie applying the tongue and groove floor boards from Old Blue after they were run through a planer to remove the old grey paint.

A small structure was built and attached to the side of New Blue to house the beer keg and keep the beer cold.

Ollie and Mike attach rough-sawn pine planks for exterior siding while Brian and Brian Lane apply roofing paper as an underlayment.

Siding has been applied and awaits log chinking after the siding has cured. Also shown it the outside bar/rifle cleaning area and the outside enclosed gun rack.

Close-up of our new and improved "Jewel" wood burning cook stove, manufactured by Detroit Stove Works.

Except for the new cook stove and a new sink countertop, the kitchen area of New Blue is an exact duplication of the kitchen in Old Blue.

Overview of the dining and card playing area of New Blue, which is an exact duplication of that in Old Blue.

Overview of the bunk area, the pantry/bar area, oil burning stove and Adder's personal lockers. All the same as Old Blue except the mattresses are new.

Shack Rules

ETIQUETTE AT THE SHACK

From the onset, the Jolly Boys believed that certain rules of conduct had to be established to assure harmony within their hunting camp because of limited space. The rules would apply to all, with no exceptions. They all thought that these rules would be instrumental in helping their camp succeed, as all knew that a great deal of effort would be needed to have up to nine hunters living together for up to nine days during the Wisconsin deer hunt. The rules addressed hygiene and behavior of the hunters, as well as other commonsense concerns, and were increased in scope as the years went by. If you are planning a new hunting camp of your own or are already involved in an established hunting camp, rule number one is to not forget the rules. Rule number two is to always remember rule number one.

SHACK RULES

- No one is allowed to return from the facilities provided outside to relieve themselves without washing their hands immediately on their return. There are never any exceptions to this hygiene rule and it will be carefully monitored.

- There will be no teeth brushing or dental flossing allowed inside the shack. This is to be done outside as there is to be no spitting in the sink area or counters that we are using for the preparation of food and for dishwashing.

- No hats are allowed to be worn at the table when eating breakfast, lunch or dinner or while playing cards. No elbows are allowed on the table while dining. Bad manners while dining will not be tolerated.

- No licking of knives is allowed. Anyone caught licking their knife and attempting to use it to take butter from the butter dish will have their hand severed at the wrist.

- Any hunter that damages camp property will be required to replace that property at his own expense.

- All poker games are limited to nickel/dime bets per pre-established shack betting rules. The maximum anyone is allowed to lose or win on any given hand on progressive card games is limited to $2.00. Stakes for cribbage games are twenty-five cents per game with fifty cents for a skunk unless the players agree beforehand to larger stakes.

- Pre-established shack rules apply to all card games. If a dispute arises and the shack rules don't address the situation, The Book of Hoyle will be consulted.

- No one is allowed to leave their clothing or personal gear on chairs and in other areas of the shack. All personal belongings have to be stowed at all times in the designated individual locker areas. Any excess clothing and gear is to be stowed in sealed plastic bins and left in the shelter of the outside wood shed.

- Boots and shoes not being worn are to be hung in the ceiling boot rack. Boots, shoes and socks are not to be left unattended on the floor.

- No one is allowed to invite a guest up to camp without the express consent of all Jolly Boys. There are no exceptions and any guest must be given the pre-approval of everyone at camp.

- Everyone is required to take their turn at doing dishes and other kitchen chores. This rule does not apply to the individual that has cooked the meal.

- Everyone is expected to share in the chores of bringing in wood, sweeping the floor, and keeping the interior of the shack clean with everything in its proper place.

- No loaded firearms are allowed inside the shack. Rifles are to be kept in the outside enclosed gun rack for everyone's safety. If a rifle becomes jammed or wet from the weather and it is necessary to bring the weapon in for maintenance, it will be done under the supervision of the Jolly Boys and inspected to be certain it is unloaded prior to bringing it into the shack.

- For the safety of everyone, all hunters hunting out of the hunting camp have to be at least 14 years of age before they are permitted to hunt with a rifle by themselves. It is permissible for a 12 year old to hunt with a rifle if they've had a hunter safety course and hunt within visual sight of their father.

- All tools and camp maintenance equipment are to be neatly stored in the attached shanty in their designated areas at all times.

- The bunk area is to be kept as cool and smoke-free as possible and it is the responsibility of all to keep the curtains to that area drawn.

- Any hunter or camp guest that has any issues with the shack rules is welcome to find a different hunting camp in which to hunt.

- It is the obligation of any hunter that receives permission to invite a guest to the hunting shack to familiarize the guest with the shack rules and to assist in enforcing the rules.

Cast of Players

If one spent the many hours necessary to read through all of the entries in the three shack logs, it would become evident why the "Jolly Boys" and their "Blue Heaven" deer camp were so familiar and beloved by so many in the Hayward and Cable area. There have been over two hundred people that have graced the interior of that little hunting shack that was situated on county forest land over the course of five decades.

The five original Jolly Boys—Marvin, Merle, Adder, Howard, and Ken—extended invitations to Clifford Bergum, Dennis Clagett, Russ Clagett, John Dunster, Brian Hanson, John Hanson, Bobby Hanson, Rob Hanson, Ollie Hanson, Sam Helms, Bob Larson, Peter Madson, Phillip Madson, Dale Nystrom, and Norm Schmickel to join them in the hunt over the course of three decades. Second-generation owners John Hanson and Dennis Clagett extended invitations to Brian Lane and Blade Lane, Phillip Rasmussen, Barry Rice, Lester Schaaf, Michael Schaaf, Nate Schmitz, Dennis Skare and several others to partake in the hunt as room in the hunting camp allowed. Third-generation owners Rob and Ollie Hanson continue that tradition by inviting others to hunt with us. The spouses of many of these hunters have also been invited to share in the experience of the hunting shack when deer season isn't in progress.

In addition to those who hunted with the Jolly Boys during deer season, a multitude of people paid a visit to the hunting shack by invitation when deer season wasn't in progress. The shack log reflects most of the Jolly Boys' visitors, including Lester and Helen Anderson, Inard "I.O."and Adah Anderson, Bobby Anderson, Tom and Betty Beckwith, Carl Benson, Romaine Berg, Clifford and Ruby Bergum with their sons Bobby and Richard, Harold and Lois Cadott, Bob and Karen Churitch, Nate DeLong, Milt and Alice Dieckman, Tom Duffy, Robert and Georgia Dunster, Chester and Edith Erickson, Harry Erickson, Hank and Toots Erickson, Adrian and Flowell Faase, Dick Gillis, Don and Elaine Gillis, Ed Gobler, Harold Gobler, Henry Gunderson, Tom and Isla Hamms, Ken and Carol Hanson, Father Bob Hanson, Arnold Hanson, Cliff Hanson, Porky Hanson, Sammy and Kathy Helms, Vern and Betty Inhoff, Clarence "Punce" Johnson, Curt Karbalis, Jim and Mary Kirby, Art Klett, Stan Knutson, Ray and Ann Lajmel, Robin Larson, Stan and Goody Laska, Wes Lindahl, Bob and Carol Longtine, Pastor Jim Mangulsen, Dennis and Delores Marquart, Metro and and Mary Maznio, Scott and Connie Miller, Jack and Colleen Moreland, Dane Nelson, Carl Nordquist, Norm and Charlotte Reisterer, Hank and Gert Rieckhoff, Walter Risberg, Art and Doris Rude, Emil and Theresa Rude, Dr. Sahs, Gordy and Jeane Ann Skamser, Harold

Tiffany, Dennis and Marlene Trembley, Michael Wetter, Blaine and Mary Wickland, Dr. Don and Margaret Willison, Dick Walker, Lyman and Edna Williamson, and Ward and Linda Williamson and many, many others who didn't sign the official shack log. Many of these former guests are now departed, but all have left their memories imbedded in those of us who remain.

Conclusion

By the fall of 2011, a stranger could walk by the former site of Camp 52 on the old fading logging road which passed by it and wouldn't suspect that a hunting camp had been situated on Sawyer County Forest lands at this location for 55 years. All the debris is gone, and nature has reclaimed the site. There is no evidence left to indicate that this was once the home of the hunting camp known as Blue Heaven, which, for at least nine days out of the year, was occupied by a group of men who called themselves the Jolly Boys.

If one continued to walk down this old logging road for about a quarter mile to the east, they would come across a relatively new hunting camp with a Schlitz beer sign hung by the buck pole, with the name "Blue Heaven" written on it. If they entered the hunting camp now known as New Blue, they would find an almost exact replica of the old hunting shack except it now was level and the roof was no longer swayback along the ridge. All of the furnishings on the interior were salvaged and are the same. The pots, pans, and dishes are the same. The walls, windows, doors, and flooring are all the same, and the interior design of the camp remains the same.

Except for the building being a few feet wider, everything is the same. Any one of the Jolly Boys of old could walk through the door of the new hunting shack and would swear that he was in the Blue Heaven of old. He would find the same traditions, the same rules, the same menu items being prepared on and in a wood-burning cook stove. He would hear the same old stories that have been told time and time again and everything would be completely familiar to him. He would be proud that the Jolly Boys legacy continues.

This is the end of my story, but it's not the end of the story. My hope is that it's just the beginning. My dream is that the visions of the Jolly Boys and their hunting camp will continue on through the generations for my sons, their children, and their grandchildren.

Recipe Index